Series created by

J. Michael Straczynski

Season by Season

NO SURRENDER, NO RETREAT

Jane Killick

B⬛XTREE

First published in the UK in 1998 by Boxtree Limited,
an imprint of Macmillan Publishers Ltd, 25 Eccleston
Place, London SW1W 9NF and Basingstoke

Associated companies throughout the world

ISBN: 0 7522 2249 X

10 9 8 7 6 5 4 3 2 1

Cover design by Shoot That Tiger!, London
Inside text by Blackjacks, London
Typeset by SX Composing DTP, Rayleigh, Essex

Printed and bound in Great Britain by
Mackays of Chatham, Kent

A CIP catalogue entry for this book is available from the
British Library

Contents

Acknowledgments

Thanks, once again, to all the wonderful people who gave their time to talk to me about their experiences on *Babylon 5*, especially Joe Straczynski, whose comments are represented here more than anyone else and therefore had to put up with more of my questions than anyone else. Thanks to Joanne Higgins for being my super-efficient contact at Babylonian Productions, to Gina and Richard for help on the Warner Bros. side of things, to my editor, Emma Mann, who remained supportive throughout, and Mum and Dad who were brilliant as always.

I also want to mention all the staff at Wolf 359 who were helpful as I was running around their convention interviewing people, and Chris O'Shea who did me a huge favour by lending me all his videos. Plus, a special thank you to David Bassom whose fault all this was in the first place.

SCRIPT TO SCREEN

Before an actor can step in front of the camera, there must be a story to tell. There must be words for him to speak, a costume for him to wear, a set for him to stand in and a camera crew to film him. All this takes a great deal of planning and co-ordination, from putting the first words of a script down on paper, through to designing and making costumes, sets, alien make-ups and organizing the filming schedule. An episode may only last forty-four minutes, but it is the result of many hundreds of man-hours.

But before there are individual episodes, there is an overall plan. This started in the late 1980s as a five-year story plan which has been added to and changed as the series has developed. The man who created the story arc, Joe Michael Straczynski, keeps his notes in a 'hodgepodge' form which he refers back to as soon as he knows there will be a new season to plan for. From there, he will develop a set of notes outlining all twenty-two stories for the season. Written down, these are little more than a few sentences describing the main thrust of an episode, such as 'Sheridan returns from Z'ha'dum and has to deal with reforming the alliance' and occasionally the major scenes, such as 'Sheridan on the bridge talking to people' from Season Four's 'The Summoning'. It may sound rather sketchy, but it is only there as a guide. A more detailed plan is locked away in Joe Straczynski's head. 'This is the Scheherazade complex,' he says. 'They have to keep you alive because if all of my notes were written down in clear and concrete form, I would be almost expendable at this point. Those aren't meant for anyone else. If you picked it up, all you would get would be the very, very broad strokes of where things are going to go. You wouldn't know the details – nor should you because if it should fall into anybody's hands, it would be all over the computer nets in twenty-four hours.'

From that, he writes an outline for the producer, John Copeland, to forewarn him and the heads of the main departments of what is to come. Also at the beginning of the season, they all sit down for what John describes as a 'post mortem' of the previous year. 'When we have these round-table discussions, we are harsher on ourselves than any critic has been in print anywhere,' he says. 'We can be pretty scathing at times and that can be good because I think that kind of honesty really has helped us to excel from season to season.'

Work can then really begin on the individual episodes, and before anything else can swing into action, there has to be a script. Sometimes, Joe Straczynski has passed on his story ideas to other writers. This happened particularly in Seasons One and Two where he would write a short outline, allowing the writer to build on those ideas and, with a certain amount of consultation, embellish them into a script. On rare occasions, the writer has come up with their own idea, as D.C. Fontana did for 'Legacies' in the first season, Laurence G. DiTillio did several times in the first two years and Neil Gaiman and Harlan Ellison have done for the fifth year. Most of the time, however, it is executive producer Joe Straczynski who writes the scripts.

Sometimes Joe will sit down at the word processor and produce a script within three days. The current record is one day to write Season Five's 'A View From the Gallery'. The result, however, represents much more than a day's work, as he will have been thinking about it long before his fingers ever touched the keyboard. 'It's like a dog chewing through a bone,' he says. 'The writing process is hardly ever clean and precise. I have a concept or a story, in which X has to happen, but the shape of it is unclear. It's like looking through a glass of the wrong prescription. If it's not quite there, then, over the next week, few days, months, whatever time I have, I'll chew through that subconsciously. Every once in a while I'll be watching a movie, or watching television, or half asleep in bed, and all of a sudden the back of my brain will go *ka-ching* [like a cash register] and something will pop up. It can be very disconcerting when Kathryn [his wife] and I are sitting having a conversation and in the middle of a sentence, I'll stop, go into fugue state, reach over, grab a piece of paper, write something down, then go back to the sentence where I'd left it off. But it means I suddenly have a piece of dialogue worked out.'

These notes are essential reminders to unlock the ideas in his head. Some writers carry a note book with them and diligently jot down any ideas they have in a neat and orderly fashion. Joe is more of a back of an envelope kind of guy. 'Yeah, unfortunately I'm not terribly well organized in that respect,' he admits. 'My office is covered in Post-it notes and scraps of paper and crap which you look at and think "this guy's office is very messy", but all those pages contain a fragment of dialogue or a description of a scene or a character note and I know where they all are, I know what every one of them means. I may pick it up and it'll have just three words on it which is designed to remind me of an entire long speech, but I only need those three words. The same way that you only need to have a few words from the speeches of Shakespeare and you know the rest of it automatically.'

From there, Joe Straczynski will occasionally write an outline which consists of no more than a page listing the beats of the episode and placing them within the six-part structure of an American television episode – the teaser, four acts and a tag. This is generally the case with a more complex episode that has several story threads. With it all set out on one page, it is easier to see that, perhaps, some material has to be taken out of Act 3 and put into Act 2. This is the usual format for writing television, especially when scripts have to be approved by producers further up the line. It will be discussed at outline stage, then a treatment will be written which breaks down the story scene by scene, and once that has been discussed and approved, the script merely fills in the details.

Joe has never worked that way, even when writing for people on other shows because he feels it stifles originality. Instead, he moves from outline to script – if he bothers to outline at all – preferring to keep the writing process a journey of discovery. 'The saying is, "the writer must surprise himself if he has any chance of surprising the audience". And so I go into each episode with the notion that no outline ever survives contact with the enemy – which is the writing of the script. In some cases, the less I have outlined, the better the script has been because you leave yourself open to the characters coming in and making suggestions and taking the show off in different directions (or that part of your brain that becomes that character for the purposes of that conversation). In many cases I'll sit down with no notes, I'll know this is an interim episode and sometimes even when it is an arc episode, if it's an important episode in the arc, I will have gone through it in my head so many times leading up to it that the actual writing of it happens in five minutes. There were several episodes this past season [Season Four] where I wrote the script in three days without any notes or outlines because I'd been thinking about it for four years.'

The result is the writer's draft. 'I'll take about a day to look at it and I'll think, can I clarify this? Tighten that? I just go through and clarify a little bit here and there and tighten all the screws, make sure the bolts are on straight and then when it's published as the first draft script, that is it. The only things that happen after that are production changes. My feeling is I wrote it right the first time and nothing much is going to be gained by going back and tinkering with it unless someone finds a massive logic flaw, which is pretty rare.'

The first person to see the script after that is producer John Copeland. He will occasionally make comments about its creative content, but his primary role is to cast a production eye over the material and point out anything which he thinks will be a problem from the production point of view. 'We're a little bit like a Chinese menu,' John explains. 'We can take one from column a, one from column b, one from column c, or we can do two from column a, two from b or we can do one from a and b and two from c. We can deal with guest cast and stunts and sets or we can deal with guest cast, extras and sets, but we can't deal with all of those four elements together. That can become very difficult for us because of the economics. If we've got lots of sets that are moving around it's hard to have three hundred extras because the extras fill the hallways when they're in between shots. Also, if we've just had an episode that's got a lot of visual effects in it, it makes it very difficult to have the next episode be a visual effects bone-crusher because we've only got so many resources.'

If there are any alterations to be made, they will be included in the first draft which is then handed out to a select number of people: the department heads, director and production manager. If there are any new characters, costumes and prosthetics, the design process will get rolling, as will the production design department if there are any new sets. All this takes place with reference to Joe Straczynski who is kept informed and consulted throughout. It is all part of what he terms 'the utility of one voice' which he tries to maintain by being involved with every aspect of the production, from the writing to the final edit and the music.

'If you look at the show and you see a Narn and you hear about the Narn culture and eventually you see the Narn homeworld, the homeworld matches what you imagine it would look like because I have sat down with everyone and made sure that the climate matches the clothing they tend to wear, which matches the skin they would happen to have, which matches the language they would happen to develop in that place. If you went to the Narn homeworld, for instance, and it looked like Minbar, your brain would say that doesn't fit, this doesn't belong with that. If you had diverse hands working on things without any kind of supervision, you would have that kind of possibility arising. My job is to work with all the departments to make sure it's consistent throughout. I try, though, not to let that go too far and be micro-managing people because nothing is won by that except to cause frustration.'

The various departments work in different ways when preparing an episode. For Ann Bruice-Aling, who is the costume designer and in overall charge of wardrobe, a meeting with Joe is the first call. 'I always make a list of questions based on each episode I read,' she says. 'Some of them are purely logistic, like how many of these guys do you think we're going to need? Then the ones that are new characters we'll talk about what he sees about the character, if there's any input he wants to give me before I attack. Then I go off and do research from a bunch of sources, period stuff and different things that I have stashed away. Like with the Drakh Emissary [in Season Four's 'Lines of Communication'], that was totally new, something that we hadn't done. We'd never seen that before and so I did a lot of research and compiled that, then I went back and talked to him about the approach. Then I do a pencil drawing and sometimes I paint them.'

John Vulich, who designs the prosthetic make-up for the alien characters, approaches his side of things in a similar way. Like Ann, he starts with the script. 'We try and glean whatever we can from the description of the character to try and work out what kind of style or demeanour for the creature or alien would work for this type of scene in the script. On another level, we try and gauge its long-term position in the script or within the arc and that involves meeting with Joe. "What do you have in store for this character somewhere down the line?" – it's something we always have to ask him. It quite frequently happens that Joe will introduce a character and he will have either a benevolent or an evil demeanour and it's very often with his style of writing that by the time you're done with that character, it's always the exact opposite of what you think he is. Deathwalker in the first season is the prime example of that and they were very particular about the design because they wanted a design that was capable of going in either direction. So it's all kind of figuring out what kind of design is suitable to this, and how it fits into the context dramatically, because ultimately what we're doing is building something that will support the story and the drama of it all. And the show's quite tricky in that way, which makes it fun actually because it's challenging when you do those kind of designs. It's easy to do a monster, but it's harder to do something that could be perceived as a monster, but later on you realize he's really your friend.'

It is much the same with set and prop design, which is part of the art department, headed by production designer John Iacovelli. 'Usually Joe is so specific in his descriptions in the script that I don't usually talk to him first,' he says. 'Although we usually show him and John either the concept sketch or the white models before we show them to the director. Joe has a very open-door policy and we run every prop by him and every set decorating spec. He's very involved with the show. It's more rare than it's frequent that he'll object or change something.'

While all the designing is going on, the production manager is working out the filming schedule. Scenes have to be grouped together to form the most efficient and practical arrangement possible. 'I sit and juggle them around,' explains Skip Beaudine, who joined as production manager in Season Three. 'I'll go through and get all the scenes that are shot in a particular set and put them together and then I move those around to fill out a day. I'll take, say, all of the Observation Dome and all of Sheridan's Office scenes and I'll put them together and that will make a day's work. Then I've got to determine what cast are in those scenes and if I'm starting any guest cast, I'll try to keep all their work within a couple of days because once they start, you pay them daily until they are finished even if they don't work.' That becomes the rough draft for the schedule which is likely to change when the director comes on board. He or she may, for example, want to spend more time on one scene than the production manager had envisaged, or cast an actor who is only available for certain days in the week.

The director, having had the script for several weeks, comes in seven days before filming is due to start for his or her official preparation period. The first job is usually casting. For a typical episode with a couple of extra characters, this will take only two or three hours, but it could take longer if they don't find anyone suitable in the first run or if it's a major character like Cartagia or Dukhat when actors can be asked back for a second audition. The rest of the week is taken up with a series of meetings, both formal and informal. The most important of these are the art department meeting, the visual effects meeting and the main production meeting, which is attended by all the departments, the director, production manager, Joe Straczynski, and producer John Copeland. 'We'll go through the script scene-by-scene,' explains John, 'discuss requirements, extras, stunts, practical effects, the blue screen's got to be in position and stuff like that. All of those things are talked about to make sure everyone's got the lay of the land for that episode.'

When considering an action scene, for example, the costume department will need to know if a character is going to be shot and therefore get a bullet hole in the costume. The logistics of the scene will also have to fit onto the set so John Iacovelli presents to the meeting scale models of every new set and a pack of scale drawings and notes. 'The key here is information,' he says. 'One of the hallmarks of the show, that has made it such a good show to work on, is that everybody knows what's going on, no one's in the dark, no one shows up and doesn't know what to expect. From the art department, we really try to show people where walls are going to be and how things are going to work.'

Then the departments will turn in their budgets to the production manager whose job it is to keep an eye on the money. It may mean that he has to negotiate with several people in order to keep costs in check. 'The art department may design a set that will cost three or four thousand dollars more than we have in the budget,' says Skip, taking an example. 'Now if I can't take it out of somewhere else, I'll go to the art department and say "OK, what can we do to cut this down?" They tell me "the director has told us he would like these certain requirements". I'll then go to the director and say "listen, we're over a little bit, where can we cut?" I just start going to the different people and we whittle it down. You kinda gotta be a psychologist in this job. You're dealing with a lot of people and everybody's working towards the same thing and you're trying to put the best possible thing on the screen. My job is to make sure that they don't go overboard. Sometimes it gets a little hard, sometimes they've got visions of something really beautiful and big and large-scale and that's not what we can do sometimes.'

John Vulich recalls one of these negotiating rounds in the fourth season when a host of Minbari extras were needed for an episode. 'I thought we'd do about thirty,' he says. 'And they go "oh I thought we'd do forty or fifty" and I go "well…" Then it was "how about sixty?" and I go "look, we can do it, we'll do sixty. Twenty of them might look wonderful, the middle twenty might look fifty/fifty type of thing where they're done quickly, and the back twenty will be really slapped together, they won't be intended for close-ups". It's always kind of negotiating things and then they'll run that by the director, "look can we shoot it this way and stage it carefully, so the really good ones are up front and the mid-ground ones in the background?" and he'll figure out how he's shooting that scene.'

One of the advantages of having the script so much ahead of time is that allows time for people to consider things and prepare. *Babylon 5* generally circulates its first draft four weeks before shooting, unlike most productions which usually manage to bring out a script little more than a week in advance. Only on the very rarest of occasions will this system trip itself up, as with the advance work done for the EarthDome corridors in the fourth season's 'Endgame'. 'That was a big set so we had to get started on it early before the budget was approved,' remembers John Iacovelli. 'The production manager came to us and said "you know, this is a big set and not much happens in it except people go back and forth, we want to cut this, we'll just do it as them coming in the doors". The art director said "we could, but we've actually bought most of that material and the set's mostly built". We have to work so fast that we're often working on things before they get approved, but in that case we had no choice. When that set was up and standing, the production manager came to us and, even though it was over the budget, he came to us – the first time he's ever done this – and said "you know, that set was really worth it". That kind of made us feel good on that one.'

While all these practical matters are being sorted out, there is a smaller scale meeting which is vital to ensuring the director is on the same wavelength as Joe Straczynski and John Copeland in terms of their vision of the episode. 'We discuss each scene, the tone of each scene, scene by scene,' explains director David Eagle. 'We talk about stuff like the dark aspect of either the entire show or the particular scene or the way in which Joe expects lines to be delivered or the way the look of that scene should be or the lighting of that scene. All of those kinds of things are discussed in great detail before I do any of my final preparation.'

The director's final preparation is essential if filming is going to go smoothly. To take David Eagle as an example, he has a meticulous approach and plans each shot in great detail. He'll write down the moves of the actors and the camera, and will often draw a diagram too. Different directors work in different ways, but David always likes to have a couple of other options up his sleeve for each scene just in case something unexpected happens – and it often does. 'I plan every shot for the entire show before we shoot the first scene,' he says. 'The way I plan my script is, I physically cut my script up with my scissors and place it together in the shooting schedule format so that my script looks like the shooting schedule. Then I write on the page next to it – if you have your script open, the right-hand side has your script, the left-hand side is the back of the previous page and it's blank – and I write all my script notes and shot lists on each of those pages. And all of that is done before I set foot on the set the first day.'

When it comes to the filming days, the first unfortunate people in are the actors who require prosthetic make-up and their make-up artists. This is usually at four or five o'clock in the morning, although it could be as early as 3am. If it is a big day for them, like in the fourth season where one of the episodes required sixty Minbari, extra people will be brought in to help put on the make-up. 'It's all planned out like a battle ahead of time,' says John Vulich who is in charge of prosthetics at Optic Nerve. 'We'll bring in eight at this time, and then the next hour bring in another eight. Then we'll bring in six at another hour and two guys go to the set to do touch-ups. It's all plotted out and oftentimes – as overkill as it might sound – I plan a lot of it on the spreadsheet of the computer. I try to plan a day out with how many there are at a given hour, how many make-ups they can do and who can I shift over to a different part of the set to do touch-ups.'

It is a similar story over at costumes, except they don't have to get up quite so early. There are two people permanently assigned to the set, a third who helps out if necessary and an additional group of wardrobe assistants brought in for the days when there are a lot of extras. 'They have to get everything ready so when the actors come in, they just go to their trailers and the clothes for the first thing they are shooting are there,' says Ann Bruice-Aling, who is in charge of costumes. 'Then they keep outer garments with them on set on the rack so they don't get any more destroyed than they need be. Then they just keep track of continuity and making sure if a cuff was unbuttoned in the beginning of the scene it's still unbuttoned at the end of the scene, or if they go back to do another take that everything is in the same position. It's very tedious, but it's also very crucial. I could never be on set, I would go nuts. You sit around for a long time doing nothing, then all of a sudden twelve thousand things need to be done in twelve seconds!'

The biggest days for costumes are when hoards of extras need to be dressed in the right clothes. Sometimes it can be quite an operation if the extras start off the day as Drazi and need to be changed halfway through to security personnel, creating the impression that there are twice as many people on Babylon 5 as have been hired. Organization on days like these is crucial, and that's where a voucher system makes life a lot easier. 'They get vouchers from central casting when they come in and that's how they get paid at the end of the day,' Ann explains. 'They have to turn their vouchers into wardrobe and they don't get them back again until they've come back to wardrobe and wardrobe gets all the pieces back. And the same thing with props. On the back of the vouchers the staff write what pieces they've given each extra so when they come back they can say "excuse me, but I know that we gave you a Psi Corps pin", and they don't get their voucher back unless they give it back.'

It is somewhat different for the art department because they are dealing with objects rather than people, although there is always a set dresser, painter and prop person on the spot to keep an eye on things. Production designer John Iacovelli is generally busy working on forthcoming episodes, but he will visit the set from time to time during filming. 'If it's a new set I usually try to be there to open up the set in the morning,' he says. 'Morning's are really critical with what happens for the rest of the day because frequently that's the first time that the DP [director of photography] and the gaffer [in charge of lighting] will have seen the set. They are so busy shooting the show that they don't often have time to come see the set ahead of time. Usually two or three days before we'll bring them over with the director and we'll show them what's going to happen. Sometimes it's the first time they've ever seen the set so there can be a lot of changes very quickly.'

Filming lasts seven days (or six as of Season Five) and the outcome of that is several hours of raw footage. The film is given to one of the show's three editors to produce a first edit and then the director comes in a couple of days later to adjust the episode to his vision. 'Usually I walk in and the show is two or three minutes long,' says director David Eagle. 'A lot of what I do is cut and trim. Some of what I do is replacing entire scenes because I don't like [the version of] the scene the editor chose and I prefer this other scene, or I want something cut out of a scene. Occasionally, especially if I'm very long, I will take a shot at doing line cuts where I'm actually cutting out lines of dialogue and trying to make it work even though that's not the way it's scripted. If I've done a really good job then Joe will accept it, if I haven't Joe will put those lines back in and cut other lines out, and that's happened both ways with me. If you're very long, if you submit a show that's two or three or nine minutes long, then Joe and John are going to cut the hell out of that show and you kind of leave yourself open. Once you see your show, it's not going to look much like what you had intended it to look like. But if you're much closer to time, I have found there's less for them to cut. If you've done a really good job and thought about the way Joe Straczynski thinks – and I've tried, and sometimes I succeed and sometimes I don't – then you're going to be very close to what your cut was.'

It has to be said, however, that most of the directors don't try and cut their episode down, preferring to present the producers with their vision in full. It is then during the producers' cut that they agonize over getting the episode down (or, on rare occasions, up) to time – and it has to be accurate to the minute, the second and the frame. Joe Straczynski and John Copeland will usually spend about a day with the editor of the episode making any changes they see fit. This is before the CGI (computer generated) effects have been done and the episode is often interspersed with sections of blank screen with a special effects shot number written on it. The length of these effects shots has to be determined at this stage and this is often achieved by Joe reading out the descriptions in the script while John enacts the flying space ships with his hands. It may sound strange, but somehow it gives them a pretty good idea of how many frames to reserve for computer graphics.

An effects spotting session usually comes next, where all the post-production CGI effects are discussed with the supervisor and the chief animator. This will be followed by an audio spotting session to sort out the music and sound effects. 'The effects editor, the sound supervisor and Christopher Franke, our composer, will sit down with Joe and I in the conference room at Babylonian Productions,' says John Copeland. 'We'll be joined by George Johnson [in charge of post-production up to and including Season Four] and we'll go through the episode on a start and stop basis, from the front to the back, and call out the in-point for music and the out-point for music. Simultaneously, we'll also be calling out specific needs for sound effects, like if there needs to be a door shut here, if there needs to be a particular sound of something we need there, and we go through the show on that basis. If the show has a lot of effects and we have a lot of slates for missing shots in there, we will wait a bit of time to allow for the shots to get dumped in.'

This is the first time composer Christopher Franke will have seen the episode, although he will have been thinking about it from having read the script. He will take this opportunity to speak to Joe Straczynski about the musical tone for the episode. 'We discuss the thematic content and we exchange ideas,' he says. 'Joe typically gives me a lot of freedom so I can come up with my own ideas. It's like a big plateau for experimentation. It's like a gigantic playground to search for new sounds or new interpretations.'

All the music is specially written for Babylon 5 on an episode by episode basis. This is the method which has been adapted by most US television shows, which have evolved a more cinematic look in recent years. Television drama previously made sparse use of incidental music, quite often using a selection of pre-recorded pieces, so every time there was a chase scene, for example, the same music would recur. Music is now much more of an integral part of a show, and Babylon 5 uses more music than most. The progress of technology has also helped composers, enabling them to use a time-coded video tape to make their music inserts accurate to a thirtieth of a second.

'The whole music studio is totally in sync with the picture,' says Chris Franke. 'Within the scene you've hundreds of little timing adjustments and ideas and it's probably more detailed than the viewer can imagine, otherwise the effect isn't there. If you want to do an accent, probably you think it would be at the same time as you see it, but the head works differently. I think the brain works a little bit quicker than it listens because sometimes you feel it's in sync even though the sound is a fraction of a second later. Sometimes the sound is effective if it's forewarning you, so it's a whole experience level of psycho-sounds, psychological hearing. A composer learns it by instinct. One day you cannot explain any more why you do it, it just feels so right.'

Part of the music is played by Chris Franke himself on electronic keyboards in his studio, the rest is recorded by the Berlin Film Symphonic Orchestra. It might seem a little extreme to go all the way to Europe for the music, but it is surprisingly efficient. Firstly, Chris has a good working relationship with the people, but more importantly it is easier to book the orchestra for short periods of time at short notice. By contrast, Los-Angeles-based orchestras tend to be booked up way in advance because of all the work provided by the Hollywood film industry. They also want to be paid for at least a three-hour session, even when the work may take only a third of that time.

The next step is to mix the episode on a dubbing stage, in order to blend all the music, dialogue and sound effects. 'That's always fun,' says John Copeland. 'It sounds so good in the mix room – big nasty speakers and we play it really loud. We mix a really dynamic sound track that is probably the most dynamic track on American television at the moment. We're barely legal we're so loud. But it's still fun. I like it when things make me vibrate!'

At the same time, the finishing touches are being put to the visual aspects of the show. The special effects have been added by this point and it is put through a digital colour balancing process. This makes the episode look uniform from scene to scene and allows for any subtle colour changes that need to be made for dramatic purposes, like changing a scene from day to night.

The title sequences and credits are added, then the audio track is laid on the colour master. Babylonian Productions make two copies, one for themselves and another for Warner Bros. which is sent off with the original ready to be broadcast.

Once that has been done twenty-two times, the season is complete.

BABYLON 5'S FOURTH SEASON

It seemed for a long time that the fourth season of *Babylon 5* would be its last. Although the door was never finally closed, the possibility hung over the production throughout the filming of Season Four, putting the original five-year story plan in jeopardy. In the light of that, it seemed foolish to carry on regardless assuming the television executives would come to their senses and renew for another season. The only option was to bring the story to a satisfactory ending, resolve the main story threads, collapse a few others and isolate the planned year five threads. It meant that creator and executive producer J. Michael Straczynski undertook, once again, to write the whole season himself.

'If you look at the structure of a given season,' he explains, 'what tends to be the case is that threads are set up within the course of a given season which [culminate] in a cliffhanger. Those threads are played out in the first four or five episodes of the new season which wraps up the previous season and begins the next arc. It's a series of overlapping bricks. If you look at a wall, you'll see the bricks aren't lined up, they're staggered, one bleeds over to the next and over to the next and so on and that's how I built *Babylon 5*. So what I had to do, therefore, was to move over those four or five episodes that would be hanging over into Season Five resolving Season Four threads. Initially, Season Four would have ended with 418 ['Intersections in Real Time'] because that's a good cliffhanger, you've got Sheridan sitting in the box. You've got him sitting there until the next season begins and you get him out of the box and you then begin the process of starting the movement that gets the Earth thread going. I had to move that forward in the storyline, so that 421 ['Rising Star'] would be a clear break. There was all this stuff that I had planned to do in year five in any event waiting to go, but it was a clean separation. If it did end on Four, viewers would walk away feeling satisfied, because we had enough material to end the storyline and the main threads have been resolved, so I could walk away feeling the time invested was worthwhile. As opposed to if we didn't get renewed and we didn't play out those threads, people would end up feeling very unsatisfied, having spent four years watching the show without getting an ending. We promised people an ending, by God, I was going to give them one.'

Perhaps it is better to watch the series without knowing this behind-the-scenes detail and perceiving the faster pace to be a natural progression. That is certainly the case if one thinks of how the series has moved from the mostly stand-alone episodes in Season One, to the first signs of movement in the story arc in Season Two and the major turns in Season Three. Season Four merely intensifies that story-telling approach. There is an enormous amount going on, particularly in the first six episodes, and sometimes it is difficult for the audience to keep up.

By episode four, for example, the tables have already turned against the Vorlons. After such a long build up from aliens of mystery, to angels and then to allies, this change in perception seems to have happened overnight. That is not to say that its inevitability was not planted in previous episodes. From Deathwalker's murder to Season Two's 'Comes the Inquisitor', when the Vorlons sent a torturer to question Delenn, their benevolence was under question. But even at the beginning of the fourth season, Delenn still believes they are on her side, believes they will persuade the League of Non-Aligned

Worlds to keep their military alliance together and that they will attempt to rescue Sheridan. When the new Kosh turns his back on her, it confirms that the Vorlons have no one's interest at heart other than their own. But to move against Kosh within four episodes of this was uncomfortably quick, especially when compared to the way Sheridan gradually built a relationship with the first Kosh back in Season Two. There were just so many issues that couldn't be addressed in the time, and Patricia Tallman, who plays Lyta Alexander, admits later in this book that she had some ethical problems over what her character was doing.

The aspect of the plot that many felt was rushed, however, was the end of the Shadow War, which came only six episodes into the season. This wasn't helped by its début showing in the USA where the broadcast of episodes four and five were separated by a two-month break, meaning it had hardly got going again before the war was over.

The original plan was to conclude the war in two and a half episodes. This was reduced to just the one, 'Into the Fire', in order to make room for events coming up later in the season. It was unfortunate because the issues that had been building over the course of more than three years were concluded within the space of forty-four minutes, hardly giving the audience time to pause for breath. There are three big movements in this episode, each highly significant, sending out resonances back into the history of the series and clarifying some of the questions that had been posed from the beginning. The first is the conflict between Shadow and Vorlon philosophies. Then the Shadows and Vorlons are confronted with their own questions, 'who are you?' and 'what do you want?' and realize they don't know the answers any more. Lorien persuades them and the other First Ones to leave the galaxy and the younger races are left on their own to embark on the new age referred to in Season One's opening narration. These steps are so momentous in the show that they deserved to have been explored in more depth.

Joe Straczynski doesn't believe anything would have been gained, fundamentally, by allowing the Shadow War to play out across three episodes as originally planned. 'All you would be adding there is extra battle sequences,' he says. 'You aren't really taking it much further because at the heart of it, the Shadow War was a philosophical disagreement.' But somehow there was not the emotional power here that accompanied other major turning points in *Babylon 5*, such as Season Three's 'Severed Dreams' in which the conflict with Earth was personalized for Sheridan through his conversation with his father and his difficulty in making a stand against his own government.

The matter is perhaps best put into perspective by actor Bruce Boxleiter, who plays Sheridan. 'I know that some fans wanted it drawn out more,' he reflects, 'but I think it's time to get it on. I actually like this season more because as the plot started happening, it got more relentless as we went, less stand-alone episodes and more arc.' That is precisely what the first six episodes are doing and, even though the pace is too relentless at times, they form a satisfying mini-sequence as the characters are propelled towards war.

Self-contained within these first six episodes are Londo's moves to rid his people of the mad Emperor that he helped put on the throne. Emperor Cartagia breathes a wonderful sense of freshness into *Babylon 5* with his eccentricity and liveliness which is in marked contrast to Londo's seriousness. But the beauty of the character is that beneath this apparently harmless, fun-loving exterior is a man of horror. He has a delusional dream of becoming a god and believes that the Shadows are able to fulfil that dream on his behalf. He is obviously quite mad, but it is not his madness that makes him a danger, it is his power. Cartagia has no qualms about sacrificing the whole Centauri population to achieve godhood for himself, and if Londo is to reverse that, he must team up with G'Kar.

Perhaps it is a leap of logic to believe that G'Kar would have left Babylon 5 to search for Garibaldi, but G'Kar was never one to sit still when something has to be done and, as he tells Marcus, he believes he can take care of himself. In any case, G'Kar and Londo have been linked at every turn and it is fate that manoeuvres them into a position where they must work together to help their respective peoples. It brings with it a great opportunity for more tension and conflict between these two, which mostly takes place in G'Kar's cell, a setting which adds an extra dynamic to the scenes. Here is G'Kar chained to the wall, beaten and tortured to a point where he should be at his weakest. Instead, he displays a resilience and pride that outshines Londo who should be in a position of strength. When Londo walks into the cell, however, he seems almost afraid of the Narn in front of him, knowing he must ask his enemy for help and that if he refuses, it will mean death and destruction for the Centauri.

Several questions set up earlier in the series are resolved within this story thread. The glimpse of Shadow vessels swarming across Centauri Prime that Londo foresaw in a dream becomes reality, with a slight costume change to make the two images match (which proves that even ambassadors have to have their coats washed sometimes!). This image originally seemed like it was a Shadow invasion, but in reality it is a greater horror because the Shadows are arriving at the request of Emperor Cartagia. Londo also discovers it was Morden who killed his beloved Adira and manipulated him to return to the Shadows at a time when he had sought to distance himself from them. It brings Londo to a greater darkness, and although he attempts to redeem himself by killing Morden, conspiring to kill Cartagia and saving Centauri Prime, he does not save himself and says that he envies Vir for having the heart to feel remorse at killing the Emperor when he himself does not.

At the end of these six busy episodes, *Babylon 5* slows down a little and starts to put into place everything that will play out in the rest of the season. 'Epiphanies' is more of a traditional *Babylon 5* episode, building expectation for what is to come. Most of the main story threads are here: Garibaldi's resignation, Bester's interest in Lyta, a reminder of the telepaths in cryonic suspension, President Clark's opposition to the station, and servants of the Shadows fleeing Z'ha'dum. 'Epiphanies' admirably answers anyone who wondered what could be left to say after the war was over, by building intrigue and excitement over a range of new story threads.

'Epiphanies' begins the middle segment of episodes leading up to the beginning of action against Earth in 'No Surrender, No Retreat'. They are somewhat of a mixture, ranging from the excellent 'Atonement' to the disappointing 'The Illusion of Truth'. 'Atonement' addresses the nagging suspicion of Delenn's involvement in the Earth–Minbari War, sometimes hinted at, but never explained. The episode works so well because Delenn is forced to face her own past mistakes, and because of the freedom science fiction allows the storyteller, she watches the whole unfortunate incident replayed in front of her. Delenn does so with Lennier at her side, finally having to admit to a close friend that she gave the order to retaliate against Earth forces, a decision which caused the deaths of many Humans and Minbari. At the same time, it gives the audience an insight into her character, how this one decision affected her life, with her guilt almost certainly explaining way she embraced prophecy

so wholeheartedly and came to Babylon 5. The perfor-
mances are also exceptional with Mira Furlan being
totally convincing as the shy, young Delenn, devoted to
Dukhat. Dukhat is played by German actor Reiner
Schone, whose accent beautifully compliments Mira's,
and whose screen presence explains why Dukhat was so
revered by the Minbari people, even after his death. A tri-
umph for the writing and production team.

'The Illusion of Truth' doesn't work nearly as well.
While the idea of exposing the media's capacity to twist
the truth is a good one, the execution of the idea doesn't
do it justice. It lacks the subtlety that would have made
ISN's news report shocking because the journalist's
motives are clear from the outset. It is also uncharacter-
istically slow, with a lengthy piece from the newscaster
at the end which, in a contemporary twentieth-century
news broadcast, would not have continued without cutting away to some other footage. It isn't a patch on the
previous ISN story, 'And Now for a Word', which is
unfortunate because it has an important message to tell
and a place in the story arc. It may look like a stand-alone
episode at first glance, but it is important to explain why
later in the series there is such opposition to Sheridan on
Earth.

The mixture continues over the next few episodes
varying in terms of achievement and tone. 'Racing Mars'
includes the explosive character clash between Sheridan
and Garibaldi that is shocking in its outcome, and all the
better for it. Marcus's and Franklin's journey to Mars
also works well with entertaining banter between the two
characters and an effective twist with the perception of
Captain Jack turning from a playful roguish character to
a tragic one. Delenn's confrontation with the Drakh in
'Lines of Communication' is more simplistic and therefore less engaging. It is not helped by the Drakh Emissary
which still looks like a monster of the week, despite

efforts to the contrary. Then there is 'Conflicts of Interest', a great turn for Garibaldi as he deals with conflicting emotions within himself when Lise, his former fiancée, arrives on Babylon 5 while tension continues between Garibaldi and Sheridan. 'Rumors, Bargains and Lies' highlights the in-fighting inside Minbari society. Then the Minbari thread reaches a satisfying climax in 'Moments of Transition' with a huge set piece for Delenn as she prepares to sacrifice herself for peace, while back on the station Lyta is forced to wear the symbol and gloves of the Psi Corps. The season then takes its second turn in 'No Surrender, No Retreat' as Sheridan moves his attention toward Earth.

The evolution of Sheridan and how this intersects with the changes in Garibaldi makes for one of the most compelling threads of the season. He is, as many characters observe, different when he comes back from Z'ha'dum. Seeing his own death brought him face to face with his own mortality and focuses attention on the life he has left. He is very aware that he is living on borrowed time, with only twenty years of Lorien's life energy to sustain him through everything he wants to achieve. It makes him more determined than he was before, more dictatorial, forging ahead without letting anyone question his actions. He decides that the Vorlon ambassador must be forced to leave and takes action without discussion; he decides the Vorlons and the Shadows must be made to face each other to end the conflict and announces it to the Alliance as a *fait accompli*; and when he has an idea of how to manipulate the other races into agreeing to let the White Star fleet patrol their borders, he carries it out without letting anyone else in on his plan.

The first two of these actions almost certainly occur because of Lorien's influence. Sheridan returns from Z'ha'dum bringing this alien with him and expects him to be accepted on his say so. The only one who greets this with some scepticism is Garibaldi who, from the very beginning, watches Lorien with a suspicious eye. This is the first hint of the tension that is to increase between these two, but at no point can Garibaldi's accusations said to be without foundation.

Sheridan's actions are questionable at many turns and this sets up a debate that continues throughout the whole of the season. The most obvious ethical question is his use of telepaths to cripple EarthForce ships, which is directly addressed on several occasions. Even as they are being activated, Franklin expresses his own moral conflict about it to a member of the Mars resistance. They are being sent into battle through no choice of their own, being used in the fight just like weapons without any respect for their Humanity. It is a terrible thing, but the alternative is much worse. If the telepaths were not to take control of the computers on the ships, the conflict would have to be solved through an exchange of firepower, killing many on both sides. The sacrifice of thirty telepaths to save the lives of thousands is the lesser of two evils. It is the same for Sheridan's decision to kill the second Kosh, to order Ranger Ericsson to lead his *White Star* crew on a suicide mission in the Shadow conflict, and to launch a military coup against President Clark to stop him destroying civilian ships.

The Sheridan who makes these difficult decisions is not quite the Sheridan who made the decision to break away from Earth in Season Three. The man who showed great doubts in attacking his own people, and even hesitated on firing on his old ship the *Agamemnon* in 'Messages From Earth', has fewer of these doubts now. This harder Sheridan, more certain of the path he must follow, is prepared to do whatever is necessary and, having already made that stand once, he finds it easier to do so again.

While Sheridan is showing his strength and resolution

as a military leader, the softer side of his character is still visible. The most significant aspect of this is his relationship with Delenn which continues to reveal his Human frailties. When he presents Delenn with an engagement ring, for example, he is full of child-like excitement and so nervous he can't quite remember where he put it. Then, when he offers her the ring, he rambles on about buying it in the Zocalo instead of explaining what this Human ritual is all about. These tender moments with Delenn help to keep the audience sympathetic towards him even when he takes a reactionary stance against Garibaldi, which he does in 'Conflicts of Interest', and when he shows harshness and indifference towards Lyta, which he does after she sends a telepathic self-destruct signal to Z'ha'dum, by asking her to move to smaller quarters. They also form a contrast and a balance with the intensity of the situations he faces, particularly towards the end of the season when he is imprisoned and tortured.

Sheridan is warned against going to Mars to meet with Garibaldi, and yet he goes. He does it because of his love for his father and perhaps because coming back from the dead and winning a war makes him feel almost invincible. It leads to his capture by the enemy and the ultimate trial for Sheridan. He must face up to everything he has done: splitting from Earth, falling in love with an alien and turning against his own government. He must find within himself the strength to resist terrible physical and mental torture through his absolute belief in the justice of his actions and his cause. 'Intersections in Real Time' is an unforgettable episode with a shocking brutality achieved without exceeding television guidelines on violence. The claustrophobic interaction between the interrogator and his prisoner gives the episode a power that could not have been achieved without such a stark setting and bold technique.

Garibaldi was the one responsible for Sheridan's

capture, and it is Garibaldi's story that excels in Season Four. Despite two major conflicts that determine the future of the galaxy and of Humanity, it this personal story that is the most gripping. The question of what happened to Garibaldi is posed at the beginning of the season, and although he is soon found and returned to Babylon 5, the question does not go away. Instead, it is metaphorically repeated over and over again, each time revealing a little bit more information to add to the intrigue. It begins with intense and startling flashes of memory that Garibaldi experiences, but seems incapable of admitting to anybody, even himself. It seems that whatever happened to him in the two weeks he was missing from the station is locked inside his head. The appearance of a Psi Cop in one of the flashbacks seems to confirm this, but does it mean he is being controlled by an outside force? Updates in his programming and glimpses into his mind, like drawing a glum face in the steam of his bathroom mirror and the Daffy Duck cartoon in which Bugs Bunny is revealed to be the animator painting Daffy's movements, suggest that he is. But by whom and for what purpose?

These questions are coupled with a change in Garibaldi, marked most notably in his resignation and his distrust of Sheridan. Whether these actions are part of his programming is difficult to determine because Garibaldi's accusations against Sheridan and his reasons for quitting have a great deal of truth about them. It leads the audience through a guessing game of what is and what is not the real Garibaldi. Whatever was done to him, part of the old Garibaldi is still visible, particularly in his relationships with others. His unease at facing Zack is one, but it is his relationship with Lise that is more significant.

How like *Babylon 5* to take a character who made a brief appearance three years previously and bring her back with a wealth of backstory to make a dramatic impact. It is much more effective than the classic television trick of bringing in the old flame for one episode and then packing her off again. Having seen Garibaldi put through so much pain in losing Lise in the first season's 'Babylon Squared', the audience expects the relationship to be restored this time. But that expectation is frustrated when he rejects her in 'Conflicts of Interest', letting her go at the end of the episode without even listening to her final message. It is only a denial of his feelings, however, and one which he cannot sustain forever. The audience's expectation is aroused for a second time when Garibaldi's work for Edgars brings him into contact with Lise again in 'The Exercise of Vital Powers'. Eventually it rewarded with the resumption of their relationship and its consummation in 'Rising Star'.

The audience's response to Garibaldi is in many ways rather contradictory and ironic. On the one hand, the viewer is willing Garibaldi to find happiness with Lise, but on the other is appalled by his moves against Sheridan. It is the betrayal of a friend that is the central event for Garibaldi in Season Four. All the emotions that are built across the season are played out in their final confrontation when Garibaldi slaps a tranquillizer pad on Sheridan's hand and watches while his enemies take him down. Clearly, it is Sheridan's trust that is betrayed, but at the same time Garibaldi is betraying himself and everything he once worked for including the loyalties and friendships of his recent past. He carries out this final act of treachery with a blank face, the face of a man whose life has been stolen by Bester.

Bester's confrontation with Garibaldi follows, and just as Garibaldi had to betray Sheridan in person to play out the drama in full, so the man who programmed Garibaldi must face him to reveal the depth of that programming. These two sequences make 'The Face of the Enemy' one of the highlights of the season, concluding one part of the story and providing answers while laying in consequences for later. For Sheridan, it is the torture he faces in 'Intersections in Real Time', and for Garibaldi it is having to return to his old friends and colleagues, knowing what terrible things he has done. It is, again, a powerful moment, pitting Franklin and Lyta's instinctive hatred of Garibaldi's actions against the memory of the friend they used to know.

The last three episodes return to the hectic pace of the beginning as Sheridan is busted out of jail and takes the lead in the final stand against Earth. Once more the speed of events leaves little time for reflection. But there is little cause to complain about the rollercoaster of events that leads to the end of Season Four. A crowd-pleasing battle, victory for our side and the resolution of all the main story threads.

Most of the fourth season had been building to this moment, from Franklin's experiments with the frozen telepaths, to forging links with the Mars resistance. Even the Shadows' alliance with the higher echelons of EarthGov is not forgotten with a fleet of Earth destroyers covered in Shadow skin adding an extra element to the battle. The fight itself is full of enough twists and turns to make it not an entirely foregone conclusion, and one that is achieved through a series of impressive CGI battle sequences. President Clark's suicide and scorched-earth policy is the final surprising turn which allows Sheridan's forces to save Earth in more ways than one. In the eyes of EarthForce administration, however, Sheridan still committed treason against his own government and is told in no uncertain terms to resign. It is a bitter-sweet moment for him because he has saved the planet, but must still face a personal punishment.

The tragedy that war brings is brought home through Ivanova who is fatally injured in the fight against the Shadow-enhanced Earth destroyers. Without this emotional core, the battle would have been over-glorified. Instead, *Babylon 5* achieves yet another emotionally charged scene as Sheridan tells her she is dying. Then, playing with audience expectations once again, Ivanova is saved at the cost of Marcus's life. The irony here is that he finally confesses that he loves her, but on the eve of his death when she cannot respond. She is left with the guilt of his sacrifice and of never being able to acknowledge his affections. There was some doubt over whether it was wise to kill off such a popular character, but without that moment of tragedy, the ending would have been too neat. Not all the problems are resolved – the dark servants of the Shadows are waiting in the wings to strike, as is the Psi Corps – but it is a happy ending for most. President Clark is replaced, Garibaldi finds love with Lise, Sheridan and Delenn get married and Londo and G'Kar are able, at last, to share a joke.

J. Michael Straczynski promised he would give us an ending to his story and, by God, he gave us one... and left just enough teasers to suggest that when renewal for a fifth season came at the eleventh hour, there was still a lot more story to tell.

NO SURRENDER, NO RETREAT

EPISODE GUIDE

1:
'Hour of the Wolf'

'The Shadows have paused in their pursuit of war and the sense of imminent change is everywhere,' G'Kar writes in his book. 'Whether it is a change for good or ill, no one can tell because no one has yet answered two very important questions: Where is Mr. Garibaldi, and what happened to Captain Sheridan?'

Delenn meets with the new Vorlon ambassador who calls himself 'Kosh', anxious about the break up of the alliance they formed to fight the Shadows. He hasn't been to council meetings to ask the League worlds to reconsider, neither will he send a rescue ship for Sheridan. 'He's bled for you, worked for you,' Delenn tells him earnestly. 'If you abandon him to die on Z'ha'dum, then I have no more respect for you.' The Vorlon replies that it is irrelevant and walks away.

Londo, back on Centauri Prime as an advisor to the Royal Court, is urged to step outside on the insistence of the Emperor Cartagia. He enters the Sand Garden where a number of others have gathered and are staring at the sky. Londo shields the sunlight from his eyes and looks up to see a fleet of Shadow vessels and fighters flying overhead, exactly how it had been foretold in his dream.

'What have you done?' Londo demands of the Emperor. Cartagia turns round with a mischievous smile, explaining quite matter-of-factly that the Shadows are guests of the Centauri Republic. Londo is incensed, he cannot understand why Cartagia has put their people on the front line like this. Cartagia

explains that the Shadows have offered to elevate him to godhood, a cause for which the Centauri people will gladly lay down their lives. Londo sees that the smile that looked at first sight like that of a mischievous child, is actually the mark of a madman.

Lyta Alexander enters Ivanova's quarters where, for the seventh night in a row, Ivanova is sitting with a glass of vodka, unable to sleep. Lyta has come to offer what the Vorlons would not: help to find Sheridan. If they go to Z'ha'dum, she believes she can telepathically block any Shadow vessels in the area, and maybe sense if Sheridan is alive. Ivanova contacts Delenn and they assemble a crew aboard one of the White Star ships.

The White Star *emerges from a jump point near Z'ha'dum and Lyta's eyes turn black as her mind makes contact with the Shadows. Ivanova sends a signal to the surface. There is no reply, but it alerts the Shadows to their presence. Ivanova moves forward, sensing something that she has felt before and at a place where her mind has been before. A pattern of six glowing Shadow eyes emerge beside the planet and lure Ivanova, Delenn and Lyta into some sort of a trance. The* White Star *suddenly turns and disappears through a jump point in an escape manoeuvre pre-programmed by Lennier. The crew snap out of their trance, but it was all for nothing. There was no signal from Sheridan, and Lyta was unable to sense him.*

Somewhere in a stone cavern on Z'ha'dum, a figure sits shrouded in a tatty piece of cloth next to a small fire. He hears an alien figure approaching and looks up. The firelight illuminates his face and reveals it is Captain John Sheridan. Sheridan looks uncertainly at the alien and wonders why he is alive.

'Well, that's the question, isn't it?' says the alien as he sits down to share the warmth from the Human's fire.

The episode opens with two questions: What happened to Sheridan and where is Garibaldi? Throughout the episode, the characters wrestle with these questions in the hope of finding an answer.

For Ivanova, hope is all she has as she clings to the slim possibility that Sheridan might be alive, even though reports suggest that he could not have survived going to Z'ha'dum. This is at a time where she needs to be strong, where she must bare the responsibility of running the station, but instead it reveals a vulnerability rarely seen in Ivanova. 'I think that it's just one more person in her life that's gone,' says actress Claudia Christian. 'She's made an emotional attachment to Sheridan. She's told herself not to because of the past, losing her parents, her brother and everybody else that has left her and I think this is just one more nail in the coffin. I don't think it was the responsibility of taking over the station when he was supposedly dead that was the difficult thing, I think it was coping with his loss as a person.'

Delenn shares Ivanova's hope, but she has one more resource to call upon, she has the Vorlons. They shared in her belief that Sheridan was important to the future and it was her who persuaded the first Kosh to save Sheridan when he jumped from an exploding shuttle in 'The Fall of Night'. She pleads with the new Kosh to rescue him a second time, but she was not prepared for his response. The Vorlon ambassador turns his back on her, explaining that Sheridan's actions at Z'ha'dum have 'opened an unexpected door'.

It destroys her respect for the Vorlons and finally shatters the image that they are a benevolent race. These beings, who present themselves as angels to other races, once seemed to have an omnipotent knowledge of the future. They saw themselves as manipulating other races to create that future, with Sheridan central to their plans. The fact that Sheridan can surprise them now reveals that they are not quite as all-knowing and unfaltering as they once appeared. It is because they don't know as much as they thought they knew, according to J. Michael Straczynski, the creative force behind *Babylon 5*. 'The thing about the Vorlons is they're very smug and they're very self-satisfied and they think they have all the bases covered,' he says. 'They think they will bring in Humans to use as cannon fodder during the war and we'll do what we're told. But they didn't count on the Human capacity for surprise, and what Sheridan does at several turns surprises them. His ability to turn the first Kosh around to help him was certainly not something they had counted on, and when he actually struck at the heart of Z'ha'dum, they saw an opportunity here to get an edge in their war of philosophy, if you will.'

With both the League of Non-Aligned Worlds and the Vorlons refusing to mount a rescue attempt for Sheridan, the only chance in recovering him from Z'ha'dum comes unexpectedly from Lyta Alexander, the Vorlon ambassador's personal assistant. Having witnessed Kosh's forthright dismissal of Delenn, she comes to see Ivanova late at night to suggest that she might be able to sense if Sheridan is still alive. It is the first indication that Lyta's loyalties are being torn between the Vorlons and the Humans. 'She is a disciple of the first Kosh, she really thinks the Vorlons are these God-like people,' explains actress Patricia Tallman. 'But there's things that they do that she doesn't understand. And Sheridan being Sheridan, she looks up to him, she cares what happens to him, she appreciates who he's been. The Vorlons not being willing to help confuses her and so she steps out a bit on her own.'

It leads Ivanova, Delenn and Lyta to embark on a desperate mission, taking the *White Star* to Z'ha'dum, even though they know it puts them at risk. Lyta uses her enhanced telepathic powers to keep Shadow forces at bay. But their power is very strong and they grip her mind, turning her eyes jet black in an effect achieved by using special contact lenses. 'The lenses are really very painful,' says Pat Tallman. 'They're completely round, and they need to be big enough so they cover the inner and outer part of my eye, so that means they're pressing under the bone. They're too big for my eyeball and we can only put them in for certain periods of time because my eyes are weeping.'

The Shadows do not resort to military force, but instead use some sort of telepathic siren song to lure the *White Star* down to the planet. Delenn and Ivanova both see images of their fathers beckoning them to land, a mystical moment suggested to the audience through dialogue rather than showing what they see. 'Oftentimes if you show too much and make it too literal, it bogs you down in details,' says writer Joe Straczynski. 'Someone says "it spoke in the voice of my father", we all hear that voice in our own heads, we don't have to go off and see this thing. It's the difference between the literal and the metaphor. Actually, they're picking up a couple of things at the same time. One is the urge to go down there and land and when Lyta says there's a voice of infinite sadness down there somewhere, that isn't coming from the Shadows, that's coming from Lorien, but she can't tell them apart at that point. The same with Delenn, they felt something was coming through very strongly. I just didn't want to get too literal about it and show it, that would take away any sense of magic or mystery or metaphor from the equation.'

While the questions about Sheridan and, to a lesser extent, Garibaldi, are being explored, a new phase of

Londo's story is unfolding on Centauri Prime. Having been recalled to the court, Londo gets to see at first hand the emperor that he helped put on the throne. This character, Cartagia, enlivens every scene he is in with a madness that has obvious parallels with the Roman Emperor, Caligula. 'Caligula is probably the most obvious comparison, hence why I had that name reflect that sound a little bit,' says Joe. 'I wanted someone who you would be very much in fear of, not because he was rampaging around screaming all the time, but because he was completely and totally arbitrary. Cartagia is governed entirely by whims, he can choose to give you a house in the kingdom or to have you killed. When he tells the guards to take G'Kar's eye, it's a whim and when they ask which one, it's a detail, "I don't care about the details". He's done with it now, he's already moved on and to have someone who is that mercurial was a fun character to get into. Most of the characters in the show tend to be more scheming and manipulative and very smart and are progressing in a clean line. Cartagia is all over the map and I liked that kind of character in the show.'

Right from the start, it is clear what Londo thinks about Cartagia. His words are very reverential, but the way he delivers them reveals he has no respect for this madman. 'The stuff that is immediately indicative of the relationship has to do with the hairstyles and that's in the very opening scene,' says Peter Jurasik, who plays Londo. 'They find Londo kind of humorous because he's wearing old style, the old fifties hairstyle. I think that was the first indication that these guys weren't going to get along... It doesn't take anybody very long to realize he's a total nut. You need to put the straightjacket on when you're moving him in the car because he's totally insane and Mollari knows that. He helped Refa put him on the throne and one of the reasons they put him on the throne was because he's a goofball. The whole fourth season is about paying back and trying to straighten out past mistakes, and that is just one of them.'

At the end of the episode, the questions that it began with remain unanswered. Only G'Kar has asked about Garibaldi and found out nothing, while the *White Star* mission to Z'ha'dum found no trace of Sheridan. Then, in the last moments, the audience glimpses of Sheridan, apparently and inexplicably alive. But how and why he is alive are two questions to which not even he knows the answers.

2:
'Whatever Happened to Mr Garibaldi?'

Sheridan wakes from a dream to see the alien looking down at him in the dim light of the tunnels on Z'ha'dum. The alien, whose name is Lorien, tells Sheridan he has been there nine days and in that time he has not eaten. 'Does blood still flow through your veins?' he asks. Sheridan reaches for the pulse on his neck and feels... nothing. 'Because,' Lorien tells him, 'you are quite, quite dead.'

Sheridan jumped into a chasm to escape the Shadows on Z'ha'dum. If he hits the bottom, then he is certainly dead and if he does not, he must be still falling and his apparent existence is just a dream. 'Unless,' says Lorien, 'you're in between.'

G'Kar's search for Mr Garibaldi brings him to a bar where he meets a trader who salvaged part of Garibaldi's lost starfury. When the trader becomes reluctant to answer G'Kar's questions, the bar owner intervenes. He orders G'Kar to leave and calls over his bouncers to impress the point. 'Such a negative personality,' says a voice from behind. G'Kar turns to see Marcus standing there with his fighting pike extended. They both move to attack and with a few blows, he and G'Kar beat back the others and escape with security alarms ringing around them.

G'Kar thanks Marcus for his help, but urges him to go back to Babylon 5 to use the station's resources to find Garibaldi. He can, he says, look after himself. But back in the bar, the owner is talking to a pair of Centauri soldiers. Soon after, G'Kar sees their shadows pass by the door and reaches for a gun under his pillow. An explosion rips the door apart and G'Kar leaps up, firing at the first Centauri that enters. A second Centauri returns fire and G'Kar falls unconscious to the ground.

Londo rushes to the throne room on a late-night summons from Cartagia and is surprised to hear that the Emperor has a gift for him. The doors open and G'Kar is brought in chained, his arms pinned to a wooden beam across his shoulders and his face bloody from being beaten. Londo looks on, torn between his need to show gratitude to Cartagia and his horror at what has been done to G'Kar.

Garibaldi paces around his cell like a lion in a cage as a disembodied voice asks him, over and over again, what happened after he left Babylon 5. 'I don't remember,' he screams in rage. He grabs at the only chair in the room, snapping off the arm and lashes out at anything and everything. Sparks fly off the metal as he strikes the door and glass shatters as he smashes the lights. Gas seeps in through vents around the room and he sinks to the floor. The cell door opens. A figure in a gas mask and a Psi Cop uniform walks in and looks down at Garibaldi's unconscious body.

Londo enters G'Kar's cell on Centauri Prime, his resolve faltering for a moment at the sight of the battered body chained to the wall. Londo tells him there will be more suffering ahead, but he believes he can save G'Kar's life if he helps to remove Cartagia from the throne. G'Kar agrees, but only if Londo will set his world free.

Lorien tells Sheridan that the only way he can escape from the in between place is to surrender

himself to death. 'I cannot create life,' Lorien says.
'But I can breathe on the remaining embers.'
Sheridan can only hope it is enough as he lays down
to die.

If one of the themes of *Babylon 5* is reaching out to catch someone from a fall*, then it would seem Lorien is the one who caught Sheridan as he fell to his death on Z'ha'dum. The presence of Kosh inside him and Sheridan's own determination to cling to life certainly play a factor in keeping him from slipping into the abyss, but it is Lorien who is the key to his survival. This alien who claims to be the oldest being alive has been alone for so long that the only thing he has to do in his life is ponder the nature of the universe. 'I tend to give my characters the questions I'm wrestling with at any given point in time,' says writer Joe Straczynski. 'In terms of the other characters, it tends to be more practical matters, matters of politics or morality, ethics. With Lorien I lumbered him with the larger questions of which came first, language or thought? Whence comes sentience? The challenge in Lorien was in not writing him as would often be the case which would be to pour out fortune cookie kinds of aphorisms. That is why I made a point of giving him questions, not answers. If you give someone answers, it becomes easy and cheap, and the answers you would be able to give in a television show would not be sufficient to the cause. I'd rather let him ask questions and let the audience answer them.

'What appealed to me about the character is, here's someone who is the oldest living being in creation we know of and he still doesn't have all the answers,' Joe continues. 'He's been working over this language versus thought thing forever and he still hasn't got it sussed out.

*See the chapter on 'The Fall of Night' in season guide #2

There's this notion that if we just live long enough, we'll figure it all out and he's proved that we don't figure it all out, we won't figure that out until we go beyond the rim, whatever that happens to be in our own cases.'

While Sheridan hovers in between life and death, G'Kar begins a personal crusade to find out what happened to Mr Garibaldi. As G'Kar says to Marcus, he does it because he has never had a friend before who wasn't a Narn. Partly because Garibaldi seems to have been forgotten in the concern for Sheridan, but mostly through a personal sense of gratitude, G'Kar sets out to find him. Leaving the sanctuary of Babylon 5 puts him in danger and prompts Marcus to follow, bringing these two characters together for the first time. 'I suddenly felt paternal in those scenes,' says Andreas Katsulas, who plays G'Kar. 'Just because of his age and my age – real ages – I just felt his impetuousness, his energy and his ambition, you know how Jason plays it and how he is in real life, actually. I felt sort of the father figure, older and wiser.'

'Working with Andreas was very nerve wracking in terms of thinking about "I was going to work with Andreas",' adds Jason Carter. 'I'm a great admirer, I think he's a brilliant actor. I think it's an incredible thing that he does considering he is completely concealed by the make-up, even his eyes are covered by contacts. There is nothing about him, his arms, everything is all make-up, it's all concealment, it's all G'Kar. His powerful humanity crosses through that and he is so expressive behind that mask, he is absolutely alive and G'Kar exists. He was fifteen years in Peter Brook's international theatre company and to have spent fifteen years in Peter Brook's company you've got to be bloody, bloody good. That's the top. The great thing about working with a great actor is the pressure's on, it makes you do good work, hopefully. Good work isn't working hard, that's the weird thing, you've just got to get all of your head in the right place. It's a commitment to the character, to what you're saying, to the situation.'

He really was quite nervous before the scene, as Andreas recalls. 'He chatters when he's nervous. Some people can't stop chattering, they have this nervous habit. I was going "yes Jason, yes Jason, it's going to be all right Jason, don't worry", and on he'd go, pacing back and forth. I actually stepped out for coffee and I came back to the chair and he was still pacing and talking!'

G'Kar is too proud to accept a bodyguard, of course, and sends Marcus away. From that moment, it was inevitable he would be captured and so begin four episodes of horror for G'Kar. He is brought into the Centauri palace in chains and Londo, who once tried to kill G'Kar at the beginning of the first season, is now horrified at what he sees. 'It's the idea of two old warriors finally and ultimately gaining respect for each other,' explains Peter Jurasik, who plays Londo. 'Finally the two feuding families say "they ain't bad, they're pretty tough if they can put up with fighting with me", so there is that grudging respect that comes with years of fighting with each other. Also Londo, while he may have blinders on, is not a stupid man and he can see the focus and respect that G'Kar has for the Narns. Londo empathizes with that because he loves the Centauri so much.'

So the two characters are thrust together again, this time on Centauri Prime. Londo sees G'Kar's presence as a way to save his people and asks G'Kar for his help. Even though G'Kar is locked in a prison cell and chained to the wall, it is Londo who appears in the weakened position. He seems almost frightened of asking G'Kar for this favour, although the Narn cannot possibly pose a physical threat to him. G'Kar merely retains his pride and is true to his cause, asking that Londo free his people in return. When they agree and Londo opens the door to leave, the light streaming in from the corridor falls across G'Kar's face like the light of salvation.

This scene is the first of many where the two former enemies face one another in the cell, forced by fate to rely on each other. 'They were great scenes to do,' says Peter Jurasik. 'They were so much fun. The isolation that was built in the scenes, they were so stark, the scenes themselves and in a real way with Andreas and I being able to focus, stay together and do the work. It really was a terrific time. Those scenes are some of my favourites.'

'You have to really find your darkest hours,' says Andreas. 'You're down and out, you're chained in a Centauri prison, there's no way out, there's a mad Emperor who's going to do you in, and you have to play that for I don't know how many episodes. That's the character's problem. The actor's problem is that Peter Jurasik is going to make long speeches and you have nothing to say and you have to sit there and listen to him!'

G'Kar's capture means that he never gets the chance to finish his search for Garibaldi. The only indication we have of what happened to Garibaldi are a couple of stark scenes of him locked in a cell ranting and raving, smashing up the lights on the walls. 'That was kind of fun, that was an ad-lib,' says actor Jerry Doyle. 'When I got into the room and saw that they had built it two inches higher than my height, it was kind of a cool little space to work in. The chair was bolted to the floor and I was supposed to use the chair to try and get the door open. When I snapped the arm off the chair I hit myself right in the nuts and I got really ticked off that I did that, so as I was doing my dialogue, I just went around and started smashing all the lights. Then the gas comes out and I hit the deck and then the director comes over and he goes "that was brilliant! I want to thank you for a lovely morning". He said "would you like to do it again?" I said "hell, yeah, I don't want to hit myself in the nuts again, but I'd like to smash the lights". This is the stuff you would love to do at home when you're having a really bad day. At work someone cleans it up for you, re-sets it and you get to smash it again.'

It answers the question of what happened to Mr Garibaldi by showing he is still alive and being interrogated by Psi Cops. But it does not explain what happened to him when he left Babylon 5 or what they want from him. It is hardly an answer at all, just a prompt for more questions.

3:
'The Summoning'

*Cartagia enters the Sand Garden with bloody hands.
'Damn him! Damn his silence!' he says, totally
exasperated. Vir and Londo look on with horror as
Cartagia casually washes his hands of G'Kar's
blood. 'I know he's my gift to you, Mollari, but if I
don't get my scream, he'll have to be killed.'
Cartagia tips the bloody water onto the roses and
goes back inside. Vir turns to Londo. There is no
doubt in his mind now that Cartagia has to be
killed.*

*Sergeant Zack Allan leads a team of starfuries to
the transport ship believed to have intercepted
Garibaldi's fighter. Before they can board it, the
ship jettisons a lifepod and explodes in a flash of
light that dies away to leave no trace of what was
inside. In the lifepod, Garibaldi lays unconscious,
strapped to a table by sheets of transparent
wrapping. 'Contact confirmed,' says a voice.
'Initiating program.' Garibaldi's eyes open and stare
vacantly into the distance.*

*Garibaldi lies in Medlab, flashes of his
programming running through his mind: going crazy
in the cell, hitting out in rage at the door and walls
that hold him. Garibaldi wakes with a start and
finds Zack standing there watching him. Zack asks
if he can remember anything about what happened.
'No,' says Garibaldi, almost too quickly. 'I don't
remember anything.'*

The White Star *travels through hyperspace in the
hope of finding more First Ones. Inside, Marcus
takes the opportunity to ask Ivanova what she plans*

to do after the war. He says he has someone special waiting for him, but she does not know it yet. 'I hope she appreciates it,' says Ivanova, ignoring the possibility that he might be talking about her. Their conversation is interrupted by a bleep from Marcus's console. It has detected a fold in hyperspace. It confuses the ship's instruments, but there is no mistaking the devastating scene confronting them through the White Star's *view panel: a mass of Vorlon ships, thousands of them, some miles across, gathered there, secretly waiting.*

Londo and Vir have been summoned to Cartagia's private sanctuary where few leave alive. Cartagia is determined to get his scream from G'Kar who is standing in front of them, chained to a post. A Centauri guard rips G'Kar's shirt from his back and strikes with an electro-whip. 'One, two, three,' Cartagia counts as each lash gains in intensity. 'Ten, eleven, twelve,' as G'Kar bears the blows with silence. 'Twenty, twenty-one, twenty-two,' as Londo mouths silently for G'Kar to scream. 'Thirty, thirty-one, thirty-two,' getting closer to the fortieth lash that will kill him. 'Thirty-seven, thirty-eight, thirty-nine,' and G'Kar screams, a long and embittered cry, and sinks to the floor.

'Everyone listen,' cries the Drazi ambassador to the crowd gathered in the Zocalo. 'Delenn and others conspiring with her are risking all of your lives by organizing an attack on the homeworld of the Shadows!' The reaction of the crowd shows they are ready to take his side.

'You cannot attack Z'ha'dum,' another alien ambassador tells them. 'No one who goes there comes back alive...' The ambassador senses he is losing the crowd's attention and turns to see what they have seen: Sheridan, the man they thought was

dead, walking into the Zocalo.

'Tell your governments,' Sheridan calls to the amazed crowd gathered before him, 'that the only man to survive Z'ha'dum sends this message: We can end this... We can fight and we can win, but only if we do it together. Can I count on you?' The cheers from the crowd tell him that he can.

Cartagia's torture of G'Kar rises to new heights of horror as the Centauri Emperor aims to crown his sadistic pleasure with a scream from the captured Narn. Londo tells G'Kar that he understands his refusal to show weakness at Cartagia's hands, but asks him to sacrifice his pride, thus revealing the similarity that underlines these two characters. 'What he was doing was asking him to compromise who he was as an individual for the sake of a bigger cause,' says Peter Jurasik, who plays Londo. 'That's what Londo's done for three seasons. Some would see it as his tragic flaw, maybe. From the beginning when we met him in "The Gathering", he talked about getting the Centauri back to where they weren't an amusement park attraction any more, and Joe has continued to push this character to a place where he sacrifices his own personal stuff for the sake of his political ambition. That's why he says to G'Kar "yeah you're going to howl, yes you're going to beg, even though it's not in your soul or your heart to do that, because you're going to do it for Narn."'

G'Kar still holds onto his dignity, withholding his scream until the last possible moment before being struck by the deadly fortieth lash of the electro-whip. It was a demanding scene for Andreas Katsulas to play. 'Knowing you're going to have to do it in rehearsal and do it again for the line up and do it again over the shoulders for the other actors,' he says. 'To do your scream from the pit of your soul that he was requiring on the fortieth lash – oh God! I'm not a method actor, I'm not trying to find a horrible scene in my life that I replay before the camera, I think the character's much bigger than that. I play it from imagination, not from real experience, so that heightens it even more for me because I can imagine worse things than have happened to me. It was draining, I was really drained and I was so happy that I was off a few episodes after that, just psychologically. I needed to get out of that, that place you go to in that dark prison.'

In the larger scheme of things, the pause in the Shadow War that G'Kar wrote about at the beginning of the season is beginning to abate as events move towards a confrontation. In preparation, Ivanova and Marcus take the *White Star* to look for more First Ones. It gives them a quiet moment to talk and, for Marcus, an opportunity to reveal he has never had a sexual relationship with a woman. 'It was quite a shock to discover that Marcus was a virgin,' says actor Jason Carter. 'I'm thirty-five years old and I've probably been a Ranger for two and a half years, but before that I was a mechanic working on mining equipment on this outlying planet – OK, so I was a thirty-three-year-old mechanic virgin? Strange.'

Or perhaps it is not so strange if you consider that, in his heart, Marcus is an incurable romantic. 'That was the conclusion,' says Jason. 'He's read a lot of literature so perhaps he has a value system that doesn't apply to the modern world; of looking for the true soul and not defiling the relationship in any way before that, having no attachments to anything or anybody. It's kind of true because he was out on an outlying mining community, so he was a bit of a loner anyway, a lone wandering knight without any training... The ironic thing about that scene is he's baring his soul to Ivanova, but she doesn't see it, or if she does, she's preoccupied elsewhere. But then again Marcus doesn't force anything at all, ever. It's all with a great deal of respect for her. I also have to add that he makes fun of Ivanova. He shows her respect, but he does make fun of her – in a loving way.'

Back on Babylon 5, Delenn is trying to build a force to strike at Z'ha'dum in an atmosphere of increasing reluctance from many of the other races, especially from the Vorlons who have turned their back on Delenn. Lyta is fully aware that they have changed their allegiances and it only takes some encouragement from Delenn for her to find the courage to confront the Vorlon ambassador about it. 'She's feeling completely betrayed, feeling used and insignificant,' says actress Patricia Tallman. 'She's not even Human any more, she's completely given up her life to being whatever they need her to be. She's a vessel for Vorlons, she carries them around and then they're going behind her back. They're not letting her in on very important decisions – not as though they would consult her – but they don't even let her know what's going on.'

It is Sheridan's return from the dead that finally turns the tables with a rallying cry that reunites the other races into forming an attack fleet. 'It's a great opportunity to come back from the dead,' says Bruce Boxleitner, who plays Sheridan. 'There's some very superstitious races here and that's a good way to do it. It's manipulative, yes, and it might be questionable as to whether a good guy would do such a thing. That's what I love about it, there's a dark side to this "Mr Good Guy", the clean-cut big guy that I'm always [playing]. He can use charisma to say "follow me".'

Sheridan's death and resurrection is a journey that has been taken by many heroes throughout the history of fiction. This pattern of storytelling was first uncovered by Joseph Campbell in his influential book *The Hero With a Thousand Faces*. Joe Straczynski is interested in the heroic myth that he described, but doesn't see it as a blueprint for Sheridan. 'I think if you hew too carefully and too closely to the formula of the heroic journey, you're going to fall down,' he says. 'Most of what works about the hero's journey is intuitive and almost subliminal, it echoes from the human spirit and not from diagrams. That's the mistake the director of the *Mad Max* movies, George Miller, made. His first two he was relying on instinct. Between *Road Warrior* and *Thunderdome* he reportedly made the error of reading Joseph Campbell and saying "oh, I see what I was doing before, now I know how to do it better", and stuck so rigorously and closely to that schematic that the third one was bloodless. So I load it up at the back of my head as a guidepost, but I don't feel any obligation to stick to it too closely. I will leave it there to inform my decisions, but not make my decisions for me.'

One of the people watching Sheridan's return from a distance is Garibaldi, although the reason he is a distant figure in the crowd has more to do with a mix up during filming than any artistic intention. Jerry Doyle, believing he was finished for the episode, decided to have his hair cut. 'I go in the make-up trailer and Kim, the girl who does the hair, said "are you sure?" And I said "yeah, it's fine, trust me, just shave my head, I want this hair off", because it was something I had been wanting to do. So she shaved my head and I said to the guys, "I'll see you Thursday", and they said, "no, we'll see you tomorrow", and I was like, "oh shit, we're going to have a little continuity problem here, aren't we?" So I went and talked to the Director of Photography, John Flinn, and he said "nah, screw it, we'll just put you in the back of the scene". They were stibbling my head and putting a little cut-out hair on there. It was like a Chia Pet*, but it worked, I guess.'

Somehow Garibaldi's distance to Sheridan fits in quite

---

*Chia Pets are novelties in the shape of animals that grow grass-like hair when you water them.

well with his later suspicion of him and Lorien. He distrusts the way Sheridan has come back like a messiah, which some people have likened to Jesus's return from the dead. Parallels have also been drawn between Lorien and God and between Garibaldi and Judas later in the season. 'There's echoes here which go to a number of different belief systems, not just Western Christianity,' says Joe Straczynski. 'There are resonances there, some of which are intentional, some of which surprise me. The character that rises up and is betrayed is an archetype and is common to virtually every culture. That is the benefit and the danger of messing with archetypes because archetypes are essentially bombs and if you start messing with them and putting them into our culture and playing with myth, it's essentially a very dangerous thing to deal with. So I've tried to be careful how I use those archetypes, but they are more Western than anything else and I'm trying to correct that for the future.'

4:
'Falling Toward Apotheosis'

The image of a Vorlon fleet appears on the monitors of Babylon 5, a recording taken moments before the destruction of Ventari Three. At the centre of the fleet is a vast ship, fifteen miles long – a Vorlon planet-killer. Energy ripples along its sides and focuses into a devastating beam at the front that obliterates the image with an intense whiteness. 'Please remain calm,' says Ivanova over the BabCom system. 'Right now, our greatest enemy is fear.'

The station is a mass of aliens and Humans trying to make their way through the crowded Customs Area. A young woman is knocked down in the scuffle and calls for help, but everyone ignores her. She is in danger of being trampled until a hand reaches down to pull her up. Her eyes brighten as she sees that her saviour is Sheridan. At his side is Lorien, constantly watching. And watching Lorien on the security cameras is Garibaldi, wondering if this alien can really be trusted.

The others can sense a certain tension between Garibaldi and Sheridan as they meet in the War Room. 'We have a security problem,' says Sheridan. 'The new Vorlon ambassador. As long as he's here, watching and reporting back, we can't do what's necessary to stop these attacks.'

Lyta tells 'Kosh' that the Humans plan to strike and offers to take him to the person who has the last remaining piece of the first Vorlon ambassador, Kosh, which could provide valuable information.

She leads the second Kosh out of the Alien Sector, mentally fighting all the while to keep him out of her thoughts. He senses something is wrong, then notices a high-voltage warning sign. But he notices it too late.

'Now!' cries Sheridan from behind some packing boxes. Lyta leaps out of the way as power surges through the circuit and arcs of electricity strike at the Vorlon like continuous white lighting, setting sparks dancing across the corridor. A security team scrambles in from outside and adds the firepower of a dozen PPG rifles. Relentless energy pounds the Vorlon's encounter suit from every direction, flashing light like a strobe over Sheridan, Lyta and Delenn's expectant faces.

The headpiece of the encounter suit explodes and an ectoplasmic column of light shoots upwards. The body of tentacled energy, like a spectral version of a Vorlon ship, circles above, looking for a way out. It sees Delenn and strikes at her. Sheridan rushes forward and is caught in the stream of energy, held helpless by its great power.

Lorien, who is watching from further back says softly, perhaps telepathically, 'now' and a glowing light – the last remaining part of Kosh – emerges from Sheridan's body. It entwines with the other Vorlon, spiralling away from the Human in a howling, screaming tangle of energy. It passes through the ceiling and into space, running in a band of light along the outside of the station until it catches up with the Vorlon ambassador's fleeing ship. It makes contact and the ship explodes, destroying all three of them.

Lorien approaches Sheridan's body and places the palm of his hand on his back. It glows softly, restoring his life for, maybe, twenty years. After that, he will simply stop.

Delenn is devastated. Has she got him back only to face losing him again? Sheridan presents her with a tiny box. She doesn't understand and so he opens it and places an engagement ring on her finger. 'Whatever time I have left,' he says, 'I want to spend it with you.' They embrace and bury their fears in the joy of the moment.

'Falling Toward Apotheosis' is predominantly about killing the Vorlon ambassador, 'Kosh 2' as he is referred to in the scripts, or 'Kosh-Vader' as he became known on the set, in deference to the evil Darth Vader of the *Star Wars* films. It is a turning point for the Babylon 5 station, making a decisive stand against the race once considered allies. Lyta is used to lure the second Kosh to where he can be attacked, something that actress Patricia Tallman was uncomfortable with. 'I had talked to Joe a couple of times about that, it seems such a drastic manoeuvre,' she says. 'The Shadows go out and kill the first Kosh and then here we are coming along to kill the second one, which doesn't make us any better than the Shadows. I really had some problems with that ethically. I realized that he had justified that in the script, that Kosh-Vader was significant in choosing planets to be destroyed. However, I wish there could be another way because resorting to that kind of destruction is – I don't know – moralistically it puts us back at that kind of level.'

'It is a very sticky ethical issue,' Joe Straczynski agrees, 'because it does qualify as murder, even though at the final analysis it wasn't them who did it, it was the last of Kosh that actually performed the act. Nonetheless, the issue remains and what I said [to Pat] was, look it's the decision you have to make in any war. What is the balance point? If you kill one person, how many do you save? We bombed Hiroshima which is a terrible thing, but did we lose fewer people than if we attempted an invasion of the Japanese mainland? It's a very difficult choice and it is both defensible and vulnerable, which are the kind of arguments that I like with this show. You can make the case that it was wrong, but if they hadn't done it, what would have been the consequences? This guy would have known their plans and the war would have never ended.'

When the time came to film the scene where Kosh is attacked and his headpiece explodes, there was more drama on the set than ended up on the screen. 'That's the day John Flinn damn near killed somebody,' Bruce Boxleitner remembers. 'I thought he was going to have a heart attack!'

The drama was the result of an accident with the explosives that could have injured the Director of Photography, John C. Flinn III, and two other camera operators, one of whom is his son, John C. Flinn IV. David Eagle, who directed the episode, remembers it vividly. 'We evacuated the set except for the three camera operators. Their job was to turn the cameras on and leave and get away. Just before they turned them on, when everybody was evacuating, all of a sudden the head explodes. John Flinn just leapt out of his chair and ran yelling and screaming "what the hell happened?" and of course everybody was very upset with our pyrotechnic folks. Somebody had touched something they shouldn't have and that was a mistake. Fortunately, no one got hurt. Stuff flew all over the place and we lost one of the Kosh heads.'

David Eagle had expected to get the shot in the can within three takes, so three Kosh heads had been prepared, but it still took an hour and a half to reset. 'There was damage to Kosh's suit,' he explains. 'They had to fill it in with putty and then paint it over. A piece of it broke off, they had to get that back on. Then, of course, they had to rewire another head and put that on. So once that was done and everybody was settled down and people were a little shaky about it, I gathered everybody together again and said "OK, let's make sure that doesn't happen again, let's go over step by step what everybody is supposed to do here". While we were talking I hear this *zzzzkshhh* and we all look over and the second head had fallen off the Kosh suit and smashed to bits on the floor. We all kind of looked at each other and thought "this is very weird, maybe Kosh doesn't want to die". We thought there was almost like a presence there, it was very spooky, very strange. By that time we were running very late and [producer] John Copeland came out and said "what the heck is going on here?" and we told him what happened and he said "how long will it take to reset up with a third head?" and we told him and he said "let's forget it, don't blow it up, we'll blow it up in post production".

'Unfortunately that's what it looks like,' David laments. 'It doesn't look the way I had intended it to look. First of all, it's just sitting there, there's no movement. If you look at those last few seconds just before the head blows up, it looks like a Kosh costume sitting on a stand. If you compare it to the scene before when Garibaldi comes to evict Kosh from his quarters and there's that fight between Kosh and Garibaldi's security forces, that was a much more realistic fight. Jeffrey [Willerth] is in the suit and he's playing Kosh and he's moving around and it all looks very real, whereas at this point where Kosh's head blows up, nobody's in the suit for safety reasons and I think you can see that. That's disappointing, but there was nothing else we could do at that point.'

Kosh is not the only one killed in the confrontation. Sheridan is brought close to death when he intervenes to stop Kosh striking at Delenn. Lorien replenishes his life force once again for, what Delenn discovers, is only twenty years. Sheridan's truncated life span explains much about his changed personality since returning from Z'ha'dum. Experiencing death made him more focused, while the prospect of only having twenty years left gives him an added urgency. His decisions to despatch Kosh and, later, to mount an attack against the Vorlons and the Shadows and subsequently against Earth, are almost dictatorial and made without hesitation. But there is still a softer side to him, brought out most obviously in his relationship with Delenn.

In this episode he tries to combat the devastating news about his reduced life span by offering her an engagement ring. There is no sense of the stoic, organized military leader here. At first, he can't remember where he put the ring, he is so excited about it. 'And very shy about it,' says Bruce Boxleitner. 'I asked Joe, saying "it's so awkward". He said "well yeah, but you're judging this on Human modern 1990s terms. You're dealing with an ancient race, the Minbari. Maybe they're very innocent in their relationships and that type of thing. How will a Human and another race be together, is it going to be a quick hop in the sack? No. Judging it all in modern Human terms doesn't work." So I say "I guess you're right..." He has a point, there. Franklin's the lover boy with all the affairs and Garibaldi with the marine [in 'GROPOS'] and with Lise. That's OK. Sheridan's is a higher love.'

'Joe likes to write it that way,' adds Mira Furlan, who plays Delenn. 'They're not just ordinary lovers, it is so much bigger than that. There is so much insecurity, especially on Delenn's part, but also on Sheridan's part, there are all these unresolved matters that complicate their lives. They come from different planets – metaphorically and physically – different worlds. I guess the element of insecurity is always there.'

Sheridan's change is one paralleled by Garibaldi, even

though this change ends up splitting them apart. This is the first episode in which Garibaldi is really up and around after returning to Babylon 5 and there is clearly something different about him. But exactly what is that difference is hard to define in these early episodes and that's how Jerry Doyle decided to play it. 'I didn't want to make the character kind of Stepfordy*, programmed or something. I didn't want to give it away that way, I just wanted to play it that his instincts or feelings were a little hyper than they normally are, a little crisper, but a little more detached at the same time. It was a weird kind of a duality to play and hopefully it came out.'

It is the duality that makes Garibaldi interesting. Much still remains of the old, familiar Garibaldi, but alongside that lies something else, often highlighted in flashbacks to his programming. The second episode posed the question 'Whatever Happened to Mr Garibaldi?' and it is a question that is still hanging in the air.

*As in the Zombielike women of the film *The Stepford Wives*

5:
'The Long Night'

Londo walks into G'Kar's cell. The Narn sits in the gloom, a ragged bandage covering the place where his eye was until Cartagia had it plucked out. Londo approaches and whispers that the time has come for them to act against the mad Emperor. G'Kar's chains have been weakened, all he has to do is distract Cartagia's personal guards for a moment and Londo will do the rest.

Cartagia sits regally at the head of the courtroom on the Narn homeworld. G'Kar staggers in, his arms chained to a wooden beam across his shoulders. Cartagia beckons Londo forward and whispers, 'I had his chains replaced by my personal guard. The others looked weak.' The smile falls from Londo's face as he watches G'Kar try to break the chains. The Narn's determination is greater than the strength of metal and the solid kirrilium links stretch, then snap. G'Kar whirls around and hits the Centauri guards with the arms of the beam.

Londo ushers Cartagia into the hallway, reaching for the assassin's tool hidden in his pocket. Cartagia is rambling on about the incompetence of his guards and, in his apprehension, Londo tells him to be quiet. 'Quiet?' shouts Cartagia indignantly and strikes Londo, sending the tool clattering to the floor. Cartagia grabs Londo in a stranglehold, then in madness tosses him away again. He whirls back round and comes face to face with Vir. Cartagia's eyes widen with shock and he looks down to his chest to see that Vir has stabbed him. 'I was going to be a god, you understand,' he says as he collapses and dies in Londo's arms.

Sheridan addresses a disparate gathering of aliens in the War Room who represent the League of Non-Aligned Worlds. He tells them that the Vorlons' next target is Coriana 6. Six billion lives will be wiped out if they don't move to stop them. He wants the entire fleet there, and – in an announcement that sends shockwaves trembling through the room – he tells them, 'I want the Shadows there as well.'

Sheridan addresses Ericsson, a Ranger in command of one of the White Star *ships, through a monitor in the War Room. As they talk, a file is sent on a sub-channel detailing information on a secret base they have established near Coriana 6. Ericsson promises the file will not fall into enemy hands. But Sheridan, his face tinged with regret, says that he wants the information to reach the Shadows. 'But Ericsson, if the information comes too easily, they won't believe it. We need them to believe it's real. Real enough to fight for, and real enough to...' Sheridan's words trail off and he sees from Ericsson's face that he need say no more. Both know it is a suicide mission.*

Back on Narn, G'Kar walks into the Centauri court as a group of Narns, drunk on victory, are smashing the place up. They want G'Kar to lead a vengeance strike against the Centauri. If their oppressors taught them anything, then it is that they need strength to lead them. 'Then you have learnt the wrong lessons,' G'Kar says. 'I did not fight to remove one dictator just to become another myself.'

Sheridan sits in his office listening to the sounds of battle being relayed from Ericsson's ship. 'Can't let them take us alive...' cries Ericsson through the distortion and sound of explosions. Then his voice softens, sensing the end has come. 'Isil-zha, veni...

in Valen's name...' The signal turns to static and Sheridan turns away. The Shadows have taken the bait.

If someone had told Londo in the first season that G'Kar would be the one to save his people, he would have probably not believed it. If that same someone had said it would be Londo who asked G'Kar to save his people, he would have almost certainly considered that person to be mad. This is how much things have changed for these two characters whose desire to save their respective homeworlds has brought them together, even though their underlying sensibilities still lie at opposite ends of the spectrum.

G'Kar, even though he is chained in a dark cell, has experienced a spiritual enlightenment in his life, while Londo has merely descended into darkness. That fundamental difference is expressed when Londo tells G'Kar his plan for killing Cartagia. G'Kar, now with only one eye, says he can see things that were invisible to him before. 'He can see your aura, he can see your soul,' says Andreas Katsulas, who plays G'Kar. 'He can see something about you, not the personality or the outer things, but he sees deep to what's thinking behind all that external stuff that you give out. So he sees way down into Londo's soul and that was something G'Kar in the first two years was unable to see about people. He can see Londo's a hollow man without a heart.'

Londo ignores this comment at the time, but it is not forgotten. In his later conversation with Vir he reflects that his remorse at killing Cartagia is the mark of a man with a good heart, implying that Londo's lack of concern makes him heartless. 'He tells that story, but unfortunately, that's not true,' says actor Peter Jurasik. 'He does have a heart or else he wouldn't be able to perceive the pain he has any more, there is no such thing. Fate and

Gods aren't kind enough to us to allow us to become totally without remorse or guilt. We can't really get fully out from under our conscience, certainly Londo Mollari can't. He would like to think he doesn't have a heart or a conscience any more, but his actions – and maybe the stuff under his actions – belie that.'

The fourth season is about Londo making amends for what he did by allying with the Shadows, trying to pull the Centauri people out of the pit he has helped put them in. His decision to kill Cartagia is partly born out of his guilt that it was his conspiracy with Refa that put the madman on the Emperor's throne in the first place. In order to carry out his act of treason, he has to build support, and he is seen doing that in a hushed meeting with other members of the court at the beginning of the episode. This scene is one continuous take with the camera moving fluidly around the outside of the table. 'That was one of my bolder moves,' says John LaFia who made his *Babylon 5* directorial début on this episode. 'I was hoping I wouldn't get cremated for it.

'I'd been doing a lot of other scenes where I had been doing a lot of coverage and I was just looking at this one and it had this kind of conspiratorial tone. Often, you feel compelled to show everybody's face constantly and I thought, I can hear what they're doing and I like the sensation of creeping around as though a listener were outside overhearing this. I did the shot and it worked so well, I figured I'll just leave it at that, so I did. You walk into someone else's playground and you never quite know how they will react to how you use their toys, but everyone seemed to be happy, so that was nice.'

Everything is leading up to Londo's assassination of Cartagia, but Vir is the one who ends up stabbing him in the heart. This was just as much a surprise to Joe Straczynski as it was to the audience. 'When I went into that script it was always going to be Londo to do the deed, but just before I got to that scene... I kind of heard Vir yelling to me in the background. I kind of turned in my head and said "what?" and he said "let me do this, because if Londo does this it'll be business as usual, he will do it and say 'OK, fine, we'll move on', whereas if I do it, there will be anguish and there will be grief and you'll get a hell of a scene of remorse from me that you would never get from Londo"... It ended up being exactly the right decision because of the scene that we got afterward with Vir having remorse, it was just a great scene for him where we see more of his character than we've seen in a long time.'

'I enjoyed killing the Emperor, he was so mean to G'Kar,' says Stephen Furst. But for his character, Vir, it is something that brings with it emotional consequences. He gets drunk afterwards to try and drown his remorse, and several episodes later is seen waking from a bad dream. It is a key moment in Vir's development away from the innocent ambassador's aide who first came to Babylon 5. 'I think that in order to grow as a person we have to experience pain,' Stephen adds. 'If everything goes right for everyone and everything falls into place as it's supposed to, we never grow as a human being and I think the same goes for a theatrical character like Vir.'

By contrast, Londo is dismissive of the whole affair. He breezes in to see Vir, having almost forgotten the act of treason, ready to move on to the next part of his plan. 'That's just the way I wanted to play it,' says Peter. 'If you watch the scene you'll see that I clap my hands a couple of times because I was trying to make it like I was calling a pet or a child, "come on, jump to it now, enough of the drinking, enough of the self pity, we have more dirt to do". But better still, not *we* have more dirt to do, *you* have more dirt to do for *me*, and he doesn't mean it in a bad way. He has this wonderful person in his life, but for the sake of Centauri and Centauri Prime he just feels like "that is your duty, Vir, you just hop to it, stop crying and let's go".'

This is a long scene, moving from the comedy of Vir's drunkenness to the tragedy of Londo's heartlessness, and finally to reflection as Vir wonders what the war was all for. It is just one example of a theatrical style that often appears in *Babylon 5*. 'All throughout the course of the show you tend to see my theatrical background peeking out of the corners,' says Joe. 'I'm always wary of it because somewhere my brain is saying "yes you have a background in theatre and you're making your audience pay for it"! But there are some scenes where that's justified and necessary. That scene needs to be that long to get to where it gets to. I could have come into that scene with him already in full remorse without the comedy at the beginning, but it all would have been one note at that point, and what interests me about a scene is the rollercoaster, where one moment you're laughing, then all of a sudden you're deeply moved by something.'

The death of Cartagia and the Centauri withdrawal from Narn is a victory for Londo, but moreover it is a victory for G'Kar and one achieved through great personal suffering. If the definition of a hero is one who is willing to sacrifice himself for others, then G'Kar is on a par with Sheridan and Delenn. Joe Straczynski agrees. 'If you really want to sit back and look at the story objectively, leaving out the expectations the television structure tends to put on us, G'Kar is certainly as much of a hero as anyone else in the show. In some ways this story is as much G'Kar's story as anyone else's and he goes through as many changes as any one else goes through. What he does in this episode, and in the ones immediately preceding, he endures almost as much – if not more in some ways – as Sheridan does. And also, like Sheridan, for the good of his people and not for any personal glory, which he actually walks away from when they try and give him the throne. That's the fun about the show, most of the characters tend to perceive themselves, one way or another, as heroes.'

6:
'Into the Fire'

*Shadow vessels shimmer into existence around
Coriana 6: Thousands upon thousands of them, so
many that the whole of space is filled with
advancing black, spidery shapes. Ahead of them, a
cluster of jump points form and the Vorlon fleet
spills out of hyperspace in a torrent that keeps on
coming.*

*Londo is drunk with joy. He has blown up the
island of Celini and destroyed the Shadow fleet
stationed there. With the death of Morden, he has
wiped out the last of their influence on Centauri
Prime. 'You're wrong,' says Vir. 'There's still one
thing left.' Vir points at Londo who suddenly
realizes the terrible oversight he has made. A Vorlon
planet-killer sails into view, blocking out the sun
and casting darkness over Centauri Prime. Londo
begs Vir to kill him. Then, suddenly, without
explanation, it sails away again.*

*All Vorlon forces are gathering around Coriana 6
where Sheridan has led the entire Alliance fleet to
make one final stand. The Vorlons seize hold of
Lyta's mind and, with eyes of glowing Vorlon-like
whiteness, she turns on Sheridan. He is caught in a
shifting pattern of energy. Lyta's eyes then turn jet
black as her mind is gripped by the Shadows, and
she turns on Delenn, entrapping her in a similar
aura of energy.*

*Sheridan faces the Vorlons who appear to him as
a woman frozen in a block of ice. 'We have wished
only the best for you,' she says. 'We have only tried
to help you.'*

Delenn faces the Shadows, coming at her one by one in the form of her friends and comrades. 'Embrace the new,' says the image of Franklin, 'Growth through pain, struggle, conflict, war.'

Sheridan circles the woman. 'You're like parents arguing in front of their kids,' he says. 'Trying to get them to take sides, not for their benefit, but for yours.'

Delenn looks into the eyes of the Shadow creature that appears as a mirror image of herself. 'What if we reject the idea that we must decide which of you is right?'

Lorien is thrown off balance by an asteroid hitting the White Star and his hands lurch deep into the auras around Sheridan and Delenn. He quickly pulls them out but the Vorlons and Shadows realize he was transmitting their debate into every mind in every ship in the Alliance fleet.

Images of a Vorlon and a Shadow creature appear on the bridge of the White Star, offering one last chance to change their minds. But Sheridan has two questions for them: 'Who are you?' and 'What do you want?' The two great powers answer with silence. 'You don't know, do you?' Delenn says scornfully. 'How can we learn who we are, what we want, if you don't even know anymore?' The great powers respond by launching a missile at the White Star, but a Drazi war ship races to intercept and is destroyed in the impact. The crew was prepared to sacrifice itself for Sheridan and Delenn, proving to the Vorlons and Shadows that the younger races will no longer be manipulated. Lorien encourages them to leave the galaxy, and they do so, taking all the First Ones with them, including Lorien himself.

The White Star heads for home. Sheridan sits with his arm around Delenn, watching as they approach

Babylon 5. 'It's a new age,' he tells her. 'We began in chaos, too primitive to make our own decisions. Then we were manipulated from outside by forces that thought they knew what was best for us... Now we're finally standing on our own.'

The end of the Shadow War so early on in the season shocked many *Babylon 5* viewers who felt it had been wrapped up too quickly. The final moves of *Babylon 5*'s great story arc were being compressed into the fourth season which, at the time, seemed like it could be the show's last. But many couldn't understand why J. Michael Straczynski couldn't have sacrificed some later episodes to allow the Shadow War to play out in full. 'For a number of reasons,' he replies. 'One, I felt it [the war] had gone about as far as it could go, also I was looking to move Season Four forward to some extent, collapse a couple of small threads. In my original notes, the Shadow War went on for about another three episodes, but it always ended the way it was going to end, so the question is do I do another couple of episodes of using pyrotechnics and blowing stuff up to make the propeller heads happy or do I move on? I was growing concerned that more and more people were thinking that the whole show was about the Shadow War, which is not the case. That was not even there in the first season, didn't even get cooking until mid way through the second season, and they thought this is the entirety of the show and it never was. I needed to shock the audience into seeing that this is about process before the war, running up to the war, the war, after the war and building the peace. Those are the five stages, so I thought let's get this done sooner rather than later and the result, of course, was a lot of fans were dumbstruck, saying "now what happens? It's got to be all downhill from there". But they failed to understand that dealing with a war on this level, what you're dealing with really are vast impersonal forces and charts on a map and on a certain level it is cold and it is impersonal. Where it gets more interesting, to my mind at least, and more personal is when a friend betrays you, because a friend knows how to hurt you. And for any dramatist – if I can use that term in relation to television – that's where the interesting stuff is, that's where the real intense stuff is. I felt by this point we've seen the Shadow vessels a hundred times and what mystery they had has been subsumed into familiarity by now and let's move on to something that is even more intense.'

There was also surprise in the way the war ended. Much of the build up suggested it would culminate in a massive battle. The White Star fleet was established, all races were brought together to fight the cause, telepaths were found to be an effective weapon and there was the promise of support from Draal and the advanced technology on Epsilon 3 (which was more likely a decoy, there instead to propel Babylon 4 back in time in Season Three's 'War Without End'). But *Babylon 5* has never been about doing what the audience expects, and as Joe Straczynski is keen to point out, the conflict was never about who has the bigger gun. 'A lot of folks wanted this to be a shoot 'em up resolution and what they were forgetting was this wasn't fundamentally a question of strengths, this was a question of philosophies and can only be resolved on a philosophical or ideological basis. I also didn't want to repeat myself because later on in the season I had brewing the Earth conflict which would be resolved by who was stronger and a whole series of major-league battles.'

Instead, Sheridan and Delenn engage in separate arguments to expose the flaws in both the Vorlons' and Shadows' philosophies. For Sheridan, it is a confrontation with a woman in an ice cube, representing the Vorlons' rigidity and inflexibility. 'I loved doing that scene because it was so strange,' says actor Bruce Boxleitner. 'That to me is science fiction right there. It was like being in *The Twilight Zone*.'

For Delenn, it was a confrontation with the Shadows who put forth their arguments using images of Ivanova, Franklin, Lennier, Marcus and even a version of herself representing their philosophy of chaos and division. 'I tried to make a distinction in how I played them,' says Mira Furlan. 'I called the other Delenn "the evil Delenn". She was this Russian female coppo in some kind of a concentration camp or something, that's how I imagined it.'

To film this, Mira had to play each Delenn separately and the two pieces of footage were merged in post production. In order for them to match, and to give her something to play against, another actress was used. 'This actress didn't have the full make-up, she only had the bone on because they only shot her from the back,' says Mira. 'When they shot the close up it would be me, and she was the other one. We had to do it a couple of times, we had to repeat that scene because it didn't succeed. It's complicated to do those scenes.'

The final breakdown in the war of ideology is when Sheridan and Delenn turn the Vorlons' and Shadows' philosophies back on themselves. When they cannot answer their own questions of who they are and what they want, it exposes their hypocrisy for all to see. 'This is a case where they had been fighting each other for so long and involved in this war of mutual attrition for so long that they forgot the point of the whole thing,' explains Joe. 'They were just as lost as those they were trying to guide and they had to be faced with that fact. Left unfettered, they would have destroyed what they were setting out to save, in the same way that we bombed villages in Vietnam to save them. You don't do it that way. We had to be shocked out of Vietnam and they had to be shocked out of what they were doing.'

Events also build to a climax on Centauri Prime where Londo is desperately trying to undo the damage done by Emperor Cartagia and lift the threat of destruction by the Vorlons. In the midst of all this, Londo discovers something very personal, that Morden was the one who killed Adira, the woman he loved. The way he has been manipulated is suddenly clear and in a great outpouring of emotion, he smashes up the room. The camera reflects his turbulent thoughts as it whirls round him in a scene that is just one continuous take. 'We had a great time doing that,' recalls actor Peter Jurasik. 'You literally only get one go at it and you're always watching out that the poor guy who was carrying the steadicam doesn't get killed! But ultimately, it was a scene I was unhappy with and dissatisfied with. If we were in a position where we had a bigger budget and more money and maybe a little more time, we maybe could have worked that scene and made that scene happen. As I've mentioned before, we have many more regrets about scenes than we have feelings of "wow, it went great".'

After such an emotional low, Londo progresses to a high as he kills Morden and delights in the fact that he has rid his world of all Shadow influences. That is, until Vir reminds him that Londo himself was touched by the Shadows. 'Good old Joe, right? Clever writing,' says Peter. 'It was a great scene to play because it was really manic, I felt like Londo was being pulled in a lot of different directions. He was drunk by the time they get around to the scene in the garden, both literally and figuratively. He literally had been drinking and he was drunk on his own compromises, he was drunk on the thought that he had just had killed Mr Morden. He goes into the garden in this state and has to do this last thing, he says to Vir "kill me", and he means it for the sake of Centauri Prime. No greater love does anyone have but to lay down his life for his people.'

Londo is only saved by Sheridan and Delenn's actions light years away, which recalls the Vorlon fleet before it can destroy Centauri Prime. At the end, as they return home to Babylon 5, they reflect on entering a new age. It is 'the third age' that the opening narration of Season One mentioned but never explained.

'The episode is really about metaphorically killing your parents,' Joe Straczynski concludes. 'The infant has to become the adult and say "I have to go on without you from now on". Very often the parent can forget that the job is to create a person, not just turn out someone who will obey you.'

7:
'Epiphanies'

Fireworks are dancing in the space around Babylon
5 as inside Humans and aliens are dancing to the
music of victory. But back on EarthDome, President
Clark has been spurred to action and has ordered
the Psi Corps to close down Babylon 5.
Permanently.

Garibaldi is shaving in the bathroom in his
quarters, steam rising from the sink and fogging the
mirror in front him. He absently draws a pair of
eyes, a nose and a straight, unsmiling mouth in the
steam. He stares at the face looking blankly back at
him for a moment and the memory of being locked
in the cell flashes back into his mind. His attention
is snapped back by the bleeping of an incoming
message. Garibaldi walks to the monitor and accepts
the incoming signal. A pattern of multicoloured
lights appears on the screen; its shifting hues
reflecting on Garibaldi's expressionless face.

Garibaldi walks into Sheridan's office. He looks
at them all – Sheridan, Ivanova and Franklin – and,
with a sense of unease, tells them, 'I've decided to
resign as head of security.'

Bester arrives on Babylon 5 with knowledge of
Clark's plans. The President has already made it
illegal to travel to the station, but that is only Phase
One of his programme. Bester promises to reveal
Phase Two, if Sheridan and the others help him find
some way to free his telepathic lover from the
Shadow implants in her brain. That means going to
Z'ha'dum.

Phase Two is intended to get military and public

opinion back on Clark's side. A Black Omega squadron, an elite Psi Corps attack force, has been ordered to intercept the squadron of starfuries patrolling the last stopover point for ships travelling from Earth to Babylon 5. The plan is to destroy the squadron and leave behind evidence linking the unprovoked murder of EarthForce pilots to Babylon 5. With that information, Ivanova leads a fleet of starfuries to the stopover point, broadcasting a warning to the EarthForce patrol. They peel away just as Black Omega begins its attack run. Both starfury squadrons return fire, catching the opposing side in a barrage of firepower until the Psi Corps ships are destroyed. The leader of the EarthForce patrol thanks Ivanova's squad, surprised that their saviours came from Babylon 5. 'Let's just say the reports of our disloyalty have been greatly exaggerated,' she replies.

The White Star *approaches Z'ha'dum just in time to see a swarm of ships flee the planet, an evacuation of Shadow allies left behind when their masters were forced out of the galaxy. Lyta senses that all that is left is a dead world. Bester is excited – that means there is no opposition to going down there and retrieving Shadow technology. But Sheridan senses trouble. 'Get us away from the planet, fast!' he orders. The ship pitches and turns, racing away from Z'ha'dum as cracks form in its surface from an eruption deep inside, breaking the planet apart in a massive explosion that shakes the* White Star.

Sheridan is suspicious about the timing of Z'ha'dum's destruction and suggests to Lyta that a telepathic probe might have set off the destruct sequence. That would have taken a very strong telepath, he tells her. Lyta all but admits she caused

Z'ha'dum to explode; maybe because of a left-over command from the Vorlons; maybe she just believed Shadow technology should not fall into anyone's hands; or maybe she just wanted to hurt Bester. Sheridan warns her that command decisions like that cannot be allowed to by-pass him. 'If this were ever to happen again,' he says, 'I would turn you over to the Psi Corps and let them turn you inside out.'

'After the war, not only did the characters need a break, but I did,' says writer Joe Straczynski. 'There is a certain amount of gear shifting that goes on. I certainly had been riding that war for some time and when I had to write this episode, it took me a while to get my feet under me again. So the next couple of episodes are laying the foundations of what's to come, and allowing me the time to change gears. "Epiphanies" does both those things. It starts the whole Minbari thread going and also deals with some left-over questions.'

Most notable is the question of Garibaldi. Since his return there had been something different about him, something clearly planted in him by the people who held him during those two weeks he was missing from Babylon 5. We see his programming being initiated and then updated when he is back on the station, but the effect on him is not entirely clear. It is all going on inside his head, and there is a hint of that in this episode when Garibaldi draws a glum face in the steam on his bathroom mirror. 'When we were doing that he [the director] said "do it like a smiley face",' actor Jerry Doyle remembers. 'I started doing a smiley face and then towards the end I trailed it off, like I'm really not happy here right now.'

It is in the middle of this scene that Garibaldi's programming is updated through an untraceable incoming message. The very next scene is his resignation speech, suggesting a causal link between these two events. And yet, in 'Face of the Enemy', Bester reveals that it was not part of his plan. It begs the question, how much was Garibaldi's resignation because he was really having doubts about his position, and how much was he being pushed in that direction? 'That's one question that's better left unanswered and unresolved,' says Joe. 'What Bester will say later on is they just pushed his natural impulses to an exaggerated level and Garibaldi is suspicious of everyone, particularly of authority figures, and in particular, authority figures who believe that they are gods or are being treated that way. So a fair amount of it is based on what he actually felt at various times, but the difference is we may all wonder if our boss is getting a little bit swell-headed about things, but very few of us would take up arms or move against them because of it. Garibaldi probably would have been concerned – and unaltered – and would probably have gone to Sheridan and voiced his concerns, but he always would have been there. In this case, he was pushed just far enough to make him take action.'

Jerry Doyle felt that at least part of his character's true feelings were behind his decision to resign. 'There's a point where you say "there's something going on here, I need to think something through, I need to make a clear-cut choice, a decision". He's going through all this stuff and he doesn't know why he's feeling what he's feeling, he's just got to do something different. It's like when I left Wall Street to become an actor*, I had a nice gig set up and I knew the business because I'd been in it for nine years. You just show up and you know your cheque's going to come in. But it was something [I had to do, I felt] I've got to make a chance for myself, I don't really know why. It probably seemed to be very stupid and foolish and all my family and friends tried to talk me out of it – much

*See the chapter on 'Survivors' in Season Guide #1

like Bruce and Dr Franklin tried to talk Garibaldi out of it, saying, "but... but... but..." on the phone, and I was saying, "you don't understand, you can't understand what I'm thinking or what I'm feeling, I can't explain it, but I just have to do it, you've got to let me do it and you've got to support me".'

It is the transitional moment for Garibaldi, making a complete break not only from his job, but also from his loyalties and his friends. Throughout this period, Zack is the only one to really support Garibaldi on a personal level. He was the first one to stand up for him on his return and that concern is evident here when he visits Garibaldi in his quarters and asks him to reconsider. 'I think there is a real bond that went on there,' says Jeff Conaway, who plays Zack. 'Zack was kind of in the middle of nowhere when Garibaldi trusted him and gave him a job. Maybe he was one of the first people who gave him a break. I think somewhere along the line Zack had a pretty good career going, screwed up by maybe decking an officer and decided to go to space to start a new life. He got to Babylon 5 and kicked around for a little while and then thought, maybe I should give this another try and Garibaldi gave him a shot. He has a deep respect for him, a loyalty, and a love for him.'

'When I was doing the scene with Jeff, trying to find the data crystals and just talking to him, I tried to keep the character banter going with him,' Jerry adds. 'Keeping it light [as if to say] "please don't let me stop dancing, because I might find myself standing still". When I turned to him to talk to him, he was kind of choked up, he had the watery eye thing going, it was like "wow, where did that come from?" I caught it and, to me, it drew the scene in a little bit closer. Then at the end of the scene when he left, I turned and all my stuff was on top of the desk and that's when I just swept it off the desk and closed the drawer, as if to say close it up and move on.'

It is also a moment for Zack to move on. The character that began as a very minor part of *Babylon 5*, grew in significance until finally getting a place in the opening titles of the fourth season. 'Epiphanies' sees him get a promotion and also approach Lyta for the first time, suggesting a possible future relationship between the two.

Lyta is also going through a transformation in her life. She destroyed her allegiances with the Vorlons when she helped to kill Kosh, but that did not endear her to Sheridan and the others. People don't trust her and she is feeling increasingly isolated. 'It didn't go the way I thought it was going to go,' reflects actress Patricia Tallman. 'Joe started writing and leading me to believe that she was a soldier of the light. She helps Ivanova, she comes up with this idea and goes to Delenn and Ivanova and says "let's go to Z'ha'dum, I might be able to feel Sheridan", without trying to reveal that she might have been Vorlon enhanced and has special gifts now. She puts herself on the line for them and nobody ever gives anything back. It's so sad. She has a scene with Zack where she says "why doesn't anyone just ask me out for dinner, go have a beer in the Zocalo? You want me to fry my mentor, but you don't want to have a pizza with me, nobody brings me flowers". It continues and continues this way. I never thought it was going to go like that.'

The end of the episode sees Zack arrive with pizza. It is a moment of hope for Lyta in an episode full of hints of a troubled future for her. She may smile in the short term when she is able to block Bester from scanning Sheridan and the others, but in the long term, it alerts him to her enhanced telepathic abilities. Suddenly he is interested in her, reminding her she has a duty to the Corps and threatening to reveal something from her past that she would prefer to keep secret. Meanwhile, her actions at Z'ha'dum in sending a telepathic probe to destroy the planet without telling Sheridan, brings her into conflict with the Captain.

'Epiphanies' is an episode in which issues begin to rise to the surface which will dominate the rest of the season. There is a lot of brooding darkness, but it is not without its lighter moments. One of the funniest is Zack's comment that, with his luck, the next person to walk onto Babylon 5 will be the second coming – followed by a trio of Elvis Presley impersonators, the first of which is actually *Babylon 5*'s art director, Mark-Louis Walters. It is, on one level, a visual pun: the Second Coming being naturally preceded by the three kings.

8:
'The Illusion of Truth'

Dan Randall stands resolutely in front of the crates
he has brought aboard Babylon 5. Sensors have
detected something unusual inside and Zack is
determined to take a look. He pulls his PPG and
Randall ducks out of the way as Zack fires, shooting
the lock off the crate. He walks forward to
investigate and finds himself staring straight at a
camera. 'I'm a reporter,' Randall announces, 'and
you just made the evening news.'

Lennier is given the job of showing Randall
around and takes him and his entourage of crew and
floating remote-controlled cameras to Down-Below,
where lurkers down on their luck line the corridors.
As they walk and talk, Dr Franklin rushes by
wheeling a woman on a stretcher who has suffered a
heart attack. Lennier introduces him to Randall as
the doctor who runs a free clinic in Down-Below.

Randall brings Sheridan and Delenn together in
the Captain's quarters and notices how close they
have become. But others, he suggests, may not
understand a relationship between Human and
Minbari. 'We will make them understand,' says
Delenn. Sheridan adds, 'There's no force in the
galaxy that can stop what we have done here
together. Nothing will stop us.'

Some days later Sheridan, Ivanova and Delenn
gather in the Captain's office to watch the special
report on ISN. It begins with shots of Down-Below
as Randall provides the commentary, 'Most of the
Human residents have been forced to live in squalid,
filthy, possibly disease-ridden areas of the station,

denied proper healthcare and sanitation.' Franklin rushes by and the image freezes on his patient. 'Any attempt at protest is cruelly put down and those responsible are sedated and taken away.'

Back in the ISN studio, Randall turns to Dr Indiri, an expert in Minbari War Syndrome. Indiri explains that many who fought in the war felt inferior to the technologically advanced aliens they were fighting and some began to see them as superior beings. 'Could Minbari War Syndrome or an unhealthy fascination with aliens, cause a person to turn against his own people, his own race?' asks Randall. Indiri agrees that, in theory, it could.

The report turns to Randall's interview with Delenn and Sheridan. They are quite obviously in love. Delenn says it may be a struggle for some people to understand about their relationship and Randall asks if it will result in a struggle against Earth. 'Of course,' replies Delenn's voice taken from an unrelated part of the interview. 'We will make them understand.' Randall suggests to Sheridan that people on Earth will be concerned that he is placing the mingling of Human and Minbari above the safety of his own world. 'There's no force in the galaxy that can stop what we have done here together,' says Sheridan. 'Nothing will stop us.'

The picture turns to Garibaldi, chatting to Randall about why he resigned from Sheridan's team. 'Sometimes, it's like he thinks he's the second coming,' he says, somewhat uneasily. 'You can't talk to him anymore, he doesn't listen. Well, that's not true, he listens to Delenn, and that other alien, Lorien, who was here for a while... I just wasn't comfortable with it anymore.'

Randall, at the ISN studios, turns to face the camera. 'Has Sheridan's self-hatred grown into a

*desire to save Humanity by making us into them?' A
picture of Delenn fills the screen. 'Delenn has shown
him the way. Half Human, half Minbari. She did it,
why can't we?... Is this the face of Humanity's
future? Sheridan's future?' He leaves the question
hanging. 'I'm Dan Randall for ISN. Goodnight.'*

' I loved that episode because I thought it was incredibly
truthful,' says Mira Furlan, who plays Delenn. 'It
spoke directly to me because I know a lot, unfortunately,
about how war propaganda works. Just as Sheridan is, I
was a target in my country of war propaganda. I was
chosen as the perfect witch that they can burn for political reasons so that everyone else gets scared and
doesn't even think of thinking any other way than what
the government wants them to think. That's what war
propaganda does in the most direct ways, they just
destroy you publicly as an example to others. It happened to many people, not only me, to the best people in
the former Yugoslavia because you had to take sides and
be a part of that war. Anybody who expressed any
doubts of the necessity of the war was punished, and
punished severely, so in that way I really felt proud of Joe
that he wrote it in the way he wrote it. There is an opinion that said there should be a Nuremberg trial for war
crimes for journalists because the war in the former
Yugoslavia began in the media. Television was spewing
hatred, spreading this evil and spreading these self-ful-
filling prophecies, saying things that then became reality.
Personally, I think the media and journalists are heavily
responsible for the war in my former country and that's
why I'm telling you this because that episode dealt with it
in a really intelligent and wonderful way.'

Joe Straczynski began as a journalist, writing for the
Los Angeles Times, the *LA Herald Examiner* and *Time,
Inc.,* among others. 'I've seen the good side of journalism

and the bad side,' he says. 'Some said this episode was an indictment of journalism. Well actually it wasn't. It was indictment of propaganda and the failure is on the part of those who don't understand there is a difference. Oddly enough, around this time, I was beginning to get word that a number of right-wing paramilitary, Posse Comitatas kind of groups were saying "Joe understands how things really are out there in the media". Oh God, they're missing the point! They're as much guilty as anybody else is.'

The episode is about manipulating the truth. The ISN crew collect a certain amount of material on its visit to the station, then deliberately use it to create a false impression. That is achieved by using a number of tricks, such as turning innocent interview responses into damning ones by pretending they were in answer to a different set of questions (recorded afterwards in a different location, you'll notice), adding a voice-over to pictures describing a different situation to the one that exists, and using an expert. Anyone can call themselves an 'expert' and attempt to give authority to a point of view and, although Dr Indiri may be genuinely experienced in treating Minbari War Syndrome, the news anchor's leading questions and request for him to make a diagnosis from several light years away make his opinion somewhat unreliable. 'The selection of quotes and the juxtaposition of quotes can be used to paint any number of pictures, which is why we must be ever vigilant about the fifth estate, which is what we call journalism over here,' says Joe. 'There is such a thing as critical thinking which means if someone brings you what they say is a fact, you must that ask them "OK, show me your work, whence came this information?" Too often we look at what we hear from the media in an uncritical fashion.'

There are several points, however, where the station leaves itself open for attack, notably with the telepaths in cryonic freeze. ISN journalist Dan Randall naturally becomes suspicious when Franklin tenses in his presence when he gets a message about them over the link. Franklin subsequently lies about them in an interview, a lie which Randall exposes by secretly discovering some of the frozen telepaths. The conclusion Randall draws is totally false, but the fact that Babylon 5 has something to hide is clear on the report. Then there are Garibaldi's comments which are a real gift to an unscrupulous journalist looking to discredit Sheridan. No tricks, no editing, no manipulation was required.

Whatever damage ISN's lies inflicts on the station, it is Garibaldi's words that really hurt. As a former member of Sheridan's staff, his words carry more credence, and cause personal as well as political damage to an old friend. Sheridan regards it as an unwarranted attack, but there is a sense of genuine concern behind what Garibaldi is saying. 'Those were deep-seated thoughts, beliefs, questions that the character had,' says actor Jerry Doyle. 'Whatever personal problems it created, it was something that Garibaldi had to do. The character can be your best friend or your worst enemy, and sometimes that can be all in the same scene.'

There is some truth in what he is saying. Sheridan *is* different since his return from alien space and has taken on a more dictatorial role, listening to only a handful of people like Lorien and Delenn. Even Bruce Boxleitner, who plays Sheridan, admits that Garibaldi has a point. 'I'm in absolute agreement. I liken him to Captain Ahab and Moby Dick in his pursuit of this Clark. Clark is sort of a Moby Dick who is at the end of the line, and Sheridan has to go through this Ahab business of getting sterner and sterner, more ruthless to get to this point. It's good because when we reach the end of the season, very apologetically he tries to explain that he is forced to resign – and not to a bad post either, as President of the

Alliance. I tried to get through that madness and tried to explain my motives. Sometimes it happens with leaders in great crisis. Our President Lincoln was a dictator at the time of the Civil War: he got rid of *habeas corpus**. Winston Churchill wasn't Mr Nice Sweetheart at the dire times of the war in Britain. It calls for desperate measures and sometimes faint hearts can be afraid, but for the ultimate good you've got to sometimes be as bad as the bad guys.'

The episode marked the *Babylon 5* directorial début of Stephen Furst, better known to viewers as Vir. It wasn't easy for him to get the gig, however, and he only succeeded after several years of pestering. 'I wanted to direct some science fiction so I kept asking them and I wouldn't let go,' says Stephen. 'Every year they told me something different. They said "we don't want to open the floodgates for actors directing", but finally I convinced them.'

In some ways, it was easier for him to be at the helm of a *Babylon 5* episode than some of the other projects he has directed because he knew the people. That familiarity also gave rise to a certain amount of playfulness among the cast, as Bill Mumy (Lennier) remembers. 'I organized an on-set walk out by the cast. The first thing we did, Stephen came over and said "OK let's make this fun", and I said "I can't deal with this kind of unprofessionalism, I'm out of here!" We all started to walk off the set for a second, just to crack him up.'

'I threw a hissy fit on the set,' adds Londo actor Peter Jurasik. 'Have you heard the term hissy fit? It means I just won't do things. I just wasn't going to come out of the trailer until the director came and chatted with me about the scene! I saw a great opportunity to rib him,

*The legal right not to be imprisoned indefinitely without being charged with a crime

he's such a great guy and a funny person to be around. And the truth of the matter is, when we did the scene, Stephen didn't say one word to me, he's so sweet. We did the scene three or four times and when the scene was over I said to Stephen "thanks, I guess you directed me, but what did we do?" He was great, he said "you didn't have to do anything, there was nothing to change so I didn't say anything".'

Stephen seems to have taken the cast banter in his stride. Asked to pick out any favourite or challenging moments for him as a director in 'The Illusion of Truth', he chooses a scene that relied on CGI effects. 'There's a funny scene with Billy and the floating cameras hitting him in the head. I loved that because it was very hard to tell because we didn't have the things there and Billy was just reacting to nothing, so when I saw it I was very pleased.'

His work must also have pleased the producers because, the following year, he came back to direct some more.

'The Hour of the Wolf': Lyta, Delenn and Ivanova sense a presence on Z'ha'dum.

The second Kosh faces his final destruction in 'Falling Toward Apotheosis'.

Sheridan ponders the rising problems with Earth in 'The Illusion of Truth'.

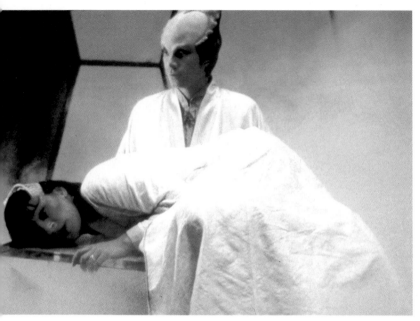

'Atonement': Delenn faces
her past in The Dreaming.

Sheridan is confronted by a Brakiri woman who believes
he is a messiah risen from the dead in 'Racing Mars'.

The Drakh Emissary from 'Lines of Communication' before his image was blurred by computer effects.

'Lines of Communication': Forell brings Delenn to meet with former allies of the Shadows.

Garibaldi surreptitiously uses a duplicate ID card to gain access to restricted parts of the station in 'Conflicts of Interest'.

The religious caste express doubts over Delenn's motives to Lennier in 'Rumors, Bargains and Lies'.

*Neroon rescues Delenn from death in the
starfire wheel in 'Moments of Transition'.*

Psi Cop Bester returns in 'Moments of Transition' to push Garibaldi further down the path he wants him to follow.

Sheridan and Marcus Encounter Earth forces in the White Star in 'No Surrender, No Retreat'.

Garibaldi meets William Edgars in 'The Exercise of Vital Powers' and cements the relationship that will lead to his eventual betrayal of Sheridan.

9:
'Atonement'

G'Kar winces as Dr Franklin inserts a prosthetic eye into the hole where his plucked-out eye used to be. G'Kar blinks and gradually a video-like image of the Medlab comes into focus. Franklin reminds him to turn the eye off at night when he takes it out to be re-charged: otherwise it will keep sending signals to his brain. 'It can work outside of me?' G'Kar asks, intrigued. He takes out the eye, turns it to face him and waves at himself.

Delenn stands before her clan in a Minbari temple. 'No Minbari has ever taken an off-worlder as lover or mate,' declares Callenn. 'It has been forbidden since our people first made contact with other species... This has caused us great concern.' He says she must enter the dreaming to discover if she is doing the right thing.

Delenn sips from a silver goblet and enters the dreaming room. Mist swirls around her as she stares into her past, to when she was a young acolyte, to when Dukhat, the leader of the Grey Council, chose her first to be his aide and later to join the Grey Council itself.

The dreaming takes her back to Minbar's first contact with Humans. Delenn, Dukhat and the rest of the Nine gather in the Grey Council Chambers where the wall has become a giant window looking out into space at the approaching fleet of ships. As is tradition, the Minbari ships have their gun ports open as a mark of respect and strength. Dukhat is alarmed. 'Close the gun ports,' he orders. But his words come too late, the Humans assume they are *about to come under attack and open fire.*

Chaos and panic spreads throughout the ship. It buckles under the onslaught, Minbari are running everywhere through smoke and debris. Delenn tries to pull Dukhat's wounded body out of the way, and as she does so he whispers to her. But his words are lost in the confusion and he dies in her lap. Another member of the Grey Council approaches her and says she holds the casting vote over whether to fight back against the Humans or not. Delenn looks up at him with grief and fury burning in her eyes. 'Follow them to their base and destroy them,' she cries. 'No Mercy!'

Delenn watches the images of herself with horror, unable to escape the truth that she was the one who started the Earth–Minbari War.

Delenn is unable to sleep in the Minbari temple, images of the dreaming keep rolling over in her mind. She sees Dukhat's last moments again, realizing he was trying to tell her something important. She decides to go back in, and take Callenn with her.

The mist swirls around them and Delenn is back on the Minbari cruiser. Dukhat whispers, and this time she leans in closer, hearing his words for the first time, 'Your heritage... You are a child of Valen.'

Delenn confronts Callenn with the facts about Valen. He was Jeffrey Sinclair, a Human who became Minbari, and whose children introduced Human DNA into Minbari society. Callenn may argue against making their race impure, but Human DNA is already in Delenn and the many other descendants of Valen. 'It doesn't matter if I marry Sheridan,' she tells him, 'my children won't be pure Minbari either way.'

Callenn says it would cause great confusion if the information was widely known, and suggests a compromise. Like in the old days, Delenn could be a peace offering to the Humans who died during the war. Delenn just smiles and walks away.

The main focus of Season Four is the aftermath of the war, but 'Atonement' takes a break from that and delves into Delenn's hidden past. 'Because it informs a lot of what follows,' says Joe Straczynski. 'The show's about process. I will go in any direction necessary: past, present and future to show you that process. This was something that a lot of people have wondered, what was Delenn's role in the war? My philosophy is that problems unaddressed don't go away, they only grow manifestly larger over time. In every person there is a key unturned, which we choose not to turn in most cases because we don't want to know what is behind that door. My job as a writer is to turn that key, open that door and whatever is inside, shove it out into the light."

Delenn is forced to confront her own past when she enters 'the dreaming', a drug-induced state given a mystical feel by the white mist swirling around her in the special room on Minbar. This caused problems on the set for Mira Furlan when she had an unexpected reaction to the dry ice. 'My body went into a shock and I had to stop shooting,' she recalls. 'You begin trembling. Your body shakes and you don't know why it's happening, it's incredibly scary. Your mind is OK and everything is OK and you don't really feel [that different]. It's kind of a pre-fainting sensation, but from that pre-fainting you begin shaking and you just can't stop. You can't stop, there's no way, it's out of your control. That was a horrifying experience because it teaches you how little control we have over our bodies. I had worked with dry ice before and I don't remember that kind of reaction. I was lying on the floor, though, and dry ice clings to the floor, so everybody standing up didn't feel it. The doctor told me that my body reacted in the sanest way possible. It's what you expire, it's CO_2, so there was a horrible lack of oxygen and my body said "no". Everybody else's body said "I hate it, but I'll deal with it". Mine didn't want to deal with it and it had nothing to do with my will.'

The shooting schedule was disrupted and some hasty re-staging was required from director Tony Dow. 'The real problem was the actor who was playing Callenn wasn't available anymore,' he says. 'He was just working those couple of days, so there wasn't an option to say, "OK, well, we'll go shoot something else and we'll come back to this tomorrow when Mira's feeling better". So I finished everything with him and there are places where it isn't Mira's hand, it's her stand-in's and there are places where it isn't her shoulder. Then there's stuff that we shot the next day with Mira where it's supposed to be part of the other guy, but it's not really him. So we had to figure out real quickly how we were going to finish the scene without showing them both together at the same time.'

When Delenn looks back into her past in the dreaming room, she sees the time before she became a member of the Grey Council, when she was chosen by Dukhat to be his aide. 'My favourite parts of that episode are young Delenn,' says Mira. 'There is this pureness and these childlike qualities that I enjoyed. It was a wonderful episode, I loved working with Reiner Schone, the actor who played Dukhat. He's a strong actor, he has a strength about him, this macho thing, he's a tall man with a huge voice, the power and charisma and so on, but he chose to play it in this playful, light way and I think it worked beautifully. It's always great when the actors play the opposite to what is written, it makes it interesting.'

Back in Season One's 'And the Sky Full of Stars',

Franklin asked Delenn what she did during the Earth–Minbari War. Her intriguing reply, 'a topic for another time' looks forward to this episode. Here is the answer to Franklin's question, that she was the one who gave the order to strike back against the Humans. Re-living that moment in the dreaming makes her face up to that responsibility. It is one that, later in the season, she says she has learnt from, but it is a private matter, something she avoids telling Sheridan.

It is a very emotive issue for the Humans and the Minbari because the war killed many on both sides, but the ever-devoted Lennier has no hesitation in standing by Delenn. 'I think it's because he loves her and wants to support her,' says actor Bill Mumy. 'I think it's also from his inner voices, his inner philosophy, his Zen-like reality which realizes you can't change it anyway, so you might as well not make her feel bad about it. You turn it around if you can because you can't take it back, so just be supportive and make her see the other side of the coin if possible.'

This whole exercise was prompted by her clan's concern over her plans to marry Sheridan and bring impurity into the Minbari race. The dreaming went back to her time with Dukhat because he believed she was a descendant of Valen. Delenn's response to her clan, that Valen introduced Human DNA into their race, makes the point that no one is truly pure, which is a strong argument against racism. 'I'm trying not to hammer it home too much,' says Joe Straczynski, 'but anyone who talks about the pure Arian race, or whatever, need only go back X number of generations and somewhere along their family tree you'll find a branch you weren't aware of. What makes us Human is our commonality. What makes us strongest is many voices raised together from different places and this episode is a nod in that direction. But, again, not trying to hammer the audience with it. No one is there saying "keeping us pure is a bad idea", it's simply not a workable idea. I try not to make our characters make a moral judgement because it then becomes preachy. I'm not saying it's good or bad, I'm saying it's ridiculous, you can't do it. That seems, to me, the more intelligent way to go.'

The episode concludes with a glimpse of Franklin and Marcus on their way to Mars in a zero gravity cargo ship. The illusion of a zero-g environment was generated by boxes on rollers wheeled in at strange angles and other assorted pieces of set dressing suspended on fishlines from the ceiling. The plan was to film the scene with a special camera that would create a 'floaty' feel. 'Unfortunately we didn't use it for that shot because it wasn't working,' says director Tony Dow. 'So we took the [ordinary] camera and there's a way to tip the camera both frontways and sideways – you can pan it and tilt it, of course with the gear hip – but there's a way to tip the camera so it's hinged. We took a piece of wood and stuck it in between the camera and the base and took the dolly and pushed it. The dolly grip was raising and lowering the dolly at random based on what the operator was telling him to do and another assistant was tipping the piece of wood under the camera and tilting it, causing it to seem like it was floating. It actually worked really well and it was quite quick.'

The scene concludes with Marcus breaking into song with Gilbert and Sullivan's *I Am the Very Model of a Modern Major General*. Jason Carter already knew the song and was determined to keep singing, even after the director said 'cut', as can be heard on the end credits. 'I delighted in it and thought "what fun",' says Jason. 'Networks have a tendency to split the screen and start advertising the next show that is coming up while the credits are rolling on the left, so there'll generally be just the music. The thing which confused some viewers in Los

Angeles was you can hear Franklin shouting "shut up, that's enough!". The LA people could hear the advertisement for the next show at the same time as "shut up!" and they got very confused as to quite what was going on, thinking it was some technical problem and they were just hearing behind the scenes in the studio! That was quite funny.'

10:
'Racing Mars'

The interview Garibaldi gave to ISN is being
broadcast over and over, adding fuel to the
propaganda war against Babylon 5. Sheridan finds
Garibaldi, hoping to talk it through, but Garibaldi
is dismissive and it just makes Sheridan more angry.
'You deliberately gave aid and comfort to the enemy
in front of billions of people,' he yells. Garibaldi is
enraged, telling Sheridan he's starting to believe his
own propaganda about being some sort of messiah
come back from the dead.

Garibaldi is stopped in the corridor by a Mr Wade
who offers him a chance to get back at Sheridan, to
stop his ego destroying all that they worked for. 'I
won't sell him out,' says Garibaldi resolutely and
walks away.

Captain Jack leads Marcus and Franklin through
the underground tunnels on Mars to the resistance
hideout. They turn the corner and are met by a
group of men who pull PPGs on them. The men take
their IDs to be checked and put a guard on them.
Marcus and Franklin sit around restlessly in the hot
atmosphere while Jack paces up and down sweating,
but refusing to take off his coat. Jack sidles up to
Franklin and pulls out a picture of his daughter,
Elysha. 'First thing I think about in the morning,
last think I think about at night,' says Jack. Franklin
flips the picture over and notes that her address is
on the back.

The men return, this time looking more
determined to use their guns. Marcus and Franklin's
DNA didn't match the ID cards. 'What'd you do

*with our contacts?' demands the first man. The
resistance leader, Number One, enters to hear their
explanation, but Franklin and Marcus have their
eyes on Jack. With a shaky hand, Jack pulls out a
gun and Marcus wheels round, striking the guard
behind him. Franklin dives for Number One, pulling
her out of the way as Jack fires. Marcus grabs a
PPG and fires back, striking Jack's shoulder. A
black, tentacled creature falls from his shoulder and
scuttles away. Jack sneaks out in the confusion.*

*Franklin studies the creature under the watchful
eyes of Number One and the other resistance
members. He believes the creature forced Jack to
betray them, switching the IDs and pulling a gun on
Number One. He had tried to tell them something
was wrong by not taking his coat off and passing on
his daughter's address in case something happened
to him. Number One contacts Jack on his comset,
telling him she understands, that the creature is
dead. 'The damned thing of it is,' Jack says from the
Martian tube car, 'they always grow back.' He
senses a tentacle reach over his shoulder and presses
the button on the thermal grenade in his hand. It
explodes, blasting Jack and the tube car to dust.*

*Sheridan approaches Garibaldi in the Marketplace
and begins to apologize for losing his temper, but a
Brakiri woman interrupts. 'You're him!' she says,
falling at Sheridan's feet. 'You died and you
returned with the knowledge of good and evil.'
Sheridan, rather embarrassed, starts to pull her up
gently, but Garibaldi grabs her and whips her away.
'For crying out loud, he's not the Pope!' he says,
shaking her violently. Sheridan pushes Garibaldi
away from her. Instinctively, he turns and throws a
punch that knocks Sheridan to the ground. Sheridan
picks himself up and glares back at Garibaldi, his*

anger now unreserved. Next time, he promises, he'll knock Garibaldi's head off.

Garibaldi seeks out Wade. 'I've changed my mind,' he says. 'I think Sheridan's lost it... I'm with you.'

'That's where I think things got interesting,' says Sheridan actor Bruce Boxleitner. 'It suddenly sparked some real interest. Garibaldi was Sinclair's good buddy and when I came there was that "do I trust you, do I not trust you?" Then we became comrades and had a really good relationship. Joe sees this and suddenly Judas starts to happen. Suddenly you're against each other. Joe always starts you one way and then you end up turning the other way. It's nice to take that relationship and dash it, turn it upside down so now they're adversaries. Actually, it's a real lovers' quarrel, good friends who are extremely hurt by what's going on.'

There were two big confrontational scenes, probably the biggest scenes the characters had had together up to that point, but it was not something the actors felt they had to work on before hand. 'I didn't talk to him much prior to it, he didn't talk to me much,' says Bruce. 'It's kind of like two fighters waiting to get into the ring. Then, of course, he had to hit me. I kept thinking, why is that? Why isn't there a fight there? In old movies he would get up and fight and Sheridan would win because ultimately he's the good guy and you're the bad guy, Garibaldi. But it doesn't work that way.'

'That was a good scene to play,' adds Jerry Doyle, who plays Garibaldi. 'Bruce is a good friend and we spend a lot of time together, play tennis together, we have good rivalries and we kind of call upon those rivalries when we have banter and we're going at each other. This went to a different level. You start to get into it and you really start to concentrate on what he's saying, you start to stare into somebody's eyes and the tennis buddy, the make-up trailer buddy starts to fall away and the words start to sink in and you get to it. Through that whole scene I was thinking "I hope I don't connect when I go to hit him", it would be like "oh my God!"'

The spur for this confrontation is Ivanova insisting Sheridan takes the day off, giving him time to brood over Garibaldi's ISN interview. It is somewhat ironic to think that Ivanova's speech about Sheridan working too hard was written by a workaholic like Joe Straczynski. 'If you look carefully at the show you will find more of my life at that moment falling into the scripts in ways that even I'm not aware of sometimes,' he says. 'I think probably there was an element of wishing somebody would come in and say "OK Joe, take the week off and we'll take care of it for you". It does pop up a lot. Certainly, if you watch all of Season Four back to back, one common thread is no one ever gets to get any sleep. They're all waking up in the middle of the night or getting up early in the morning or there's someone banging on their door. Everyone keeps lamenting "why can't I get one good night's sleep around here?" which has been my lament for the entire fourth season: "I just want one good night's sleep". So a lot of me leaks in and when I catch it I take it out. Sometimes I'm not even aware of it until someone says "do you notice you were doing this?" and I go "oh shit!"'

The focus of the episode, though, is Marcus's and Franklin's trip to Mars. It's a fun pairing and each time these two get together, their banter seems to get more lively. 'I think Joe's really good at watching us when we're out having lunch,' suggests Richard Biggs, who plays Franklin. 'Sitting around waiting for the next shot, he sees personalities that might be interesting on stage and Jason and I seem to click. We're both a little hyper and we kind of feed off each other, the characters are opposites. A real, cerebral, intellectual doctor and this real physical type of a guy, Marcus, who's a very spiritual, very innocent kind of a guy, but at the same time can hold his own, danger is what he's used to. So it's two total opposites and it just clicks.'

'It's an interesting pairing,' agrees Jason Carter, who plays Marcus. 'We come from almost polar opposites in the way the two characters view the world. Franklin is quite pragmatic and methodical and ordered and I would say that Marcus has much more of a dynamic, unpredictable and intuitive energy that will strike suddenly in one direction. He is playing I-spy with Franklin and Franklin turns around and Marcus has gone like a cat. Bang! There was danger and the next thing he's coming round the corner with Captain Jack trussed up from behind. He's always alive and the rest is just froth. Never distracted, even though playing.'

The humour is just part of *Babylon 5*'s rich tapestry. Here, it contrasts very nicely with the emotional tension between Sheridan and Garibaldi. Director Jesús Treviño believes it is crucial in providing variety and keeping interest alive. 'In this particular case I think the key to it was casting,' he says. 'The gentleman that we got to play Captain Jack [Donovan Scott] was just a very funny actor and he understood what his role was and he could go from that to the darker side when he blows himself up. Clearly when you have someone like him it becomes infectious and you can carry the humour along. There was one moment that Jason's character was reading his lines as if he was someone out of Monty Python and it brought the whole the crew into hysterics. It was the kind of thing I would have loved to have been able to say, "come on, Joe, let's really do this", because we know all the *B5* fans are going to get this. But that's where I think you don't want to get people out of what the story is that you're telling because then you break that fourth wall, you break that suspension of disbelief – but he can be very funny.'

One of Jason Carter's behind the scenes comedy routines became somewhat of an inspiration for one of the elements of the story in 'Racing Mars'. When Marcus and Franklin arrive on Mars they discover that no one knows anything about the Shadow War, just as many people in the modern world are ignorant of some of the major events on our own planet. 'It is also a very subtle – almost so subtle to the point of not perhaps getting the point across – take on American myopia,' says Joe Straczynski. 'Jason Carter used to make the joke about problems in Europe by doing his version of the evening news which was "today there was a big problem in Germany, but no Americans were involved, so moving on…" If we weren't personally involved, we don't much care. And if Mars wasn't directly involved, they didn't much care.'

The other humorous thread in 'Racing Mars' is Delenn inviting Sheridan to join her in a Minbari ritual to discover each other's centres of pleasure – while a group of other Minbari listen from outside the bedroom. 'It's not my favourite material, but I have to do it,' Bruce Boxleitner confesses. 'It helps round out the character in the bigger picture. Even if it's not the best part of the character's arc, it still takes that certain edge off for the audience. Even if it's nonsensical, it helps lighten it, so this character isn't all brooding anger.'

'Whenever something comes up like this or Londo's genitalia, I just don't want to know where it comes from,' adds Joe. 'It would be confronting that part of myself that actually thinks up this stuff, I'd rather just not know. So the Minbari ritual of pleasure, I'm just in denial about it. Every so often my brain will just go into infarction and I will look at and go, you're just out of your mind! But on one level, it does actually make some kind of sense, in some cultures there are rituals that do similar things.

Oddly enough, when I was in the UK, I had to change rooms at one point because apparently there was this wedding going on at the hotel and there's this tradition that the mother of the bride has to sleep in the room below the daughter, which I'd never heard of before. God knows what she would hear on the floor below, but apparently that is what they do and I was kind of thinking, well that's kind of Minbari of them. This is slightly exaggerated, but one can almost make an argument for it and I thought, let's just embarrass Sheridan a little bit because he didn't deal as well with that as he might have.'

11:
'Lines of Communication'

'Damn it, Susan, I've got it!' says Sheridan, bursting into Ivanova's quarters in the middle of the night. He hardly gives her a chance to change out of her dressing gown before he's taking her to the War Room to explain his new idea. She is going to be their weapon against ISN's propaganda, he tells her. The Voice of the Resistance, broadcasting the truth to combat the lies.

Franklin addresses the resistance leaders on Mars, appealing to them to lend their support to Sheridan's campaign against President Clark. If they come to trust Babylon 5, to carry out instructions without question, then Sheridan guarantees Mars will be recognized as an independent state when it is all over. It is enough to gain their support and a dinner invitation from Number One.

Delenn journeys in the White Star to the borders of Minbari space where reports say their allies from smaller worlds are being attacked. They arrive just as a Pak'ma'ra ship is destroyed. One of the Minbari crew, Forell, pulls a gun on Delenn and demands that she listens to what the attackers have to say.

A creature that calls itself the Emissary of the Drakh moves through the corridors of the White Star bringing a sense of darkness that light shies away from. It urges Forell to tell his story so he explains how his family was expelled from its home by the warrior caste and died from exposure before they could reach the nearest town. He says that the Drakh are prepared to be their allies to make sure the warrior caste do not take control of Minbar. In return, the Drakh – whose planet has been destroyed – will set up home on the borders of Minbari space. Delenn agrees to consider the Drakh's plan, but as soon as the Emissary leaves, she turns on Forell. 'Sheridan and I defeated the Shadows, drove them and their allies from Z'ha'dum which was then destroyed. They worked for the Shadows, Forell. And you brought me right into the middle of them.'

Energy starts to build up on the Drakh ships as they engage their weapons. The White Stars activate jump engines and break off in all directions. The Drakh fleet responds with a barrage of fire, hitting Delenn's ship as it escapes into hyperspace. Sparks fly from the consoles and a metal beam falls from the ceiling, striking Forell and knocking him to the floor. Forell, in his last moments before he dies, apologizes to Delenn for thinking the Drakh could help their people. 'No,' says Delenn. 'I'm sorry, Forell. I should have never been away this long.'

Delenn orders the fleet to turn round and finish what it started. Jump points appear all around the Drakh mother ship and White Stars emerge, firing. They strike at the Drakh fighters engaging in a dog fight of criss-crossing beams of energy and exploding vessels. The White Star moves across the mothership, firing repeatedly, creating small explosions on its surface as it tries to escape to the jumpgate. The White Star moves faster, flips round and fires continually back at the Drakh ship, burning through the hull until a chain reaction of explosions escalates into a ball of fire.

Delenn returns to Babylon 5 to tell Sheridan that she is leaving for Minbar. She must try to stop the *splintering caste system escalating into civil war. It is the best for both of them, she says. 'What is left requires that you be dangerous, and I think you would be more comfortable doing that if I were not here.'*

After an extended period standing in Sheridan's shadow, Delenn steps back into the light and resumes the same tough stance she showed when standing up to the Grey Council and organizing a fleet to protect Babylon 5 against Earth. In 'The Illusion of Truth' she was seen lovingly at Sheridan's side, in 'Racing Mars' she enticed him with the Minbari ritual of pleasure, but here she tells him never to forget who she was and what she can do. 'I talked to people, especially women at conventions, who were very dissatisfied with the direction Delenn was taking,' says actress Mira Furlan. 'I think the female audience craves to see a strong woman who is presented in a good way, a positive way, not as an evil horrifying witch which is what is usually done. To see Delenn being this little lamb, this tiny little lost girl, got on their nerves and I can completely understand that. So Joe told me "enough of that sweet Delenn, let's go back to the tough Delenn". He told me "I wrote that sentence for you, 'never forget who I am or what I can do'". The beauty of Delenn is she can be anything and I think it makes her so much more complicated.'

Later in the episode Delenn tells Sheridan that he would find it easier to do what he has to do if she was not there. This idea is somewhat foreshadowed when Delenn leaves to deal with a number of attacks on the border of Minbari space. Sheridan is suddenly inspired to strike back against ISN's propaganda broadcasts and gets Ivanova out of bed in excitement. 'He's like a schoolboy with a new idea,' says actor Bruce Boxleitner. 'I always try to keep that kid in him who's over excited. He was the child who could never sit still in class, they had to tie him to his chair or something!'

'And she says "you don't even notice that I'm wearing a nightgown?"' adds actress Claudia Christian. '"What am I, chopped liver?" That was kind of funny because you see the element of her being a viable woman, thinking, "God, have I taken this job so far that I am now just a masculine entity?" It would have been fun to carry that through and see her try to be a little more feminine at work after that.'

Delenn's mission to the borders of Minbari space brings her into contact with the Drakh, a race who were allies of the Shadows. This emphasizes one of the themes of the season, that the war has left a legacy that has to be dealt with. The Drakh Emissary was described in the script as a servant of the darkness who caused lights to dim as it neared them as if sucking the life and light out of everything it passes. In the event, an effect was added in post production that turned it into a blurred, indistinct figure. 'I had everything darken when he comes near it because I was so burned with the "Infection" situation and the "Grey 17..." thing,' explains Joe Straczynski. 'I said I don't want to do another obvious guy in a rubber suit, so let's keep this dark and shadowy. Of course, it was shot nice and bright and also the paint job on the actual face wasn't what I wanted it to be, it was the wrong colour and it ended up looking like a mask instead of looking like a breather unit. I thought, well look, these guys worked for the Shadows, they would have some access to Shadow technology and we know the Shadows can phase in and out of appearance. Why can we not make the logical extension that they have adapted a system which keeps them blurry a little bit? They really can't be seen clearly and thus become more ominous and thus more frightening to the average passer-by.'

The man underneath the costume was a Frenchman, Jean-Luc Martin. 'He was a really nice guy, a good actor too,' remembers Bill Mumy, who plays Lennier. 'He was from the *Circ du Solei* and a handsome man under that costume, you wouldn't believe it. He got burnt very badly one day by an electrical shock, not scarred, but really shocked bad and singed. He had to endure a terrible, hard, physical costume with all these wires running into it. Then, on the other hand, [we had an actor who] had to be a Minbari and he couldn't remember his lines at all and he was really making me angry. I mean, I'll be honest about that, if you're hired as a guest actor to come in and do a day's work, learn your lines, man. There's a lot of people, a lot of hungry actors out there who can do it, so don't show up for the interview if you can't do it. And if you can do it and you get the job, you better show up and do it. This guy – nothing personal against him – but he was like take twenty and this other poor man is wearing this horrible heavy suit and he's hitting his mark and saying his lines and doing these great physical things and we had to keep doing it over and over again because this other guy couldn't remember his lines. It was a torturous day.'

While the end of the Shadow War was bringing new enemies to light, it also allowed attention to turn to other issues that had been bubbling under the surface. The issue of President Clark and the strong resistance to his rule on Mars comes together with Marcus's and Franklin's appeal to resistance leaders. This is something Franklin is not used to doing. He is taken out of the sphere of being a doctor and has to draw on other parts of his personality to persuade the resistance to back Sheridan. 'Joe really made a point to get the doctor out of the Medlab,' says actor Richard Biggs. 'You get to see the doctor out of his element, which I always felt would be more interesting. I think Dr Franklin is in control when he is in the Medlab, no matter how hectic, no matter how under pressure or under the gun he may be, I think he is used to that and thrives on that. But get him out of the Medlab and you put him in a place where he isn't quite as comfortable, doing things that he isn't used to doing, going to Mars and talking to the resistance, trying to talk to them into coming over to the Babylon 5 side, working with us. You're going to find much more interesting stories, a much more interesting character.'

During his visit to Mars he finds something unexpected, a relationship with Number One. In the past, his relationships had been fly-by-night. Love was brief in 'The Long Night' when the patient he developed feelings for left for Earth, and his encounter with Cailyn in 'Walkabout' was only a stop-off on his journey to find himself. Now Richard Biggs feels his character had come to a point where he could handle more than a casual relationship. 'I think it also had a lot to do with what he had been through. I think he could live more for the moment. He was planning so far ahead and trying to get things done and get twenty-five hours out of the day, but now he's more interested in dealing with the moment. When Joe wrote that all that we have is the next moment, I think that's one of the things that the doctor learned after going through that huge ordeal about getting stabbed and slowly bleeding to death and seeing himself.'

It is Marcus, however, that encourages Franklin not to shy away from Number One, telling him to touch passion when it comes his way. 'God, that's a good speech,' says Jason Carter. 'That's very confusing for Marcus to be saying that. I had to deal with Marcus's point of view that he was quite detached from the realm of sexual lust and desire and had raised himself above the physical pleasure plane, as it were. So to have him recommend that Franklin do that is almost full of regret and very telling of a certain emptiness in Marcus's soul. Marcus is looking for a powerful flame, but sees Franklin staring at the candle and goes "hey, go for the candle, there's little enough flame as it is".'

Says Joe, 'I've never seen one guy's lack of experience prevent him from giving another guy advice on his love life.' The sentiments Marcus expresses to Franklin are just as much about himself as they are about the doctor. There is part of him that is also longing to be touched by passion which puts a melancholic tone on the final scene as Marcus sits on guard duty with the sounds of Franklin and Number One's passion in the background.

12:
'Conflicts of Interest'

Zack approaches Garibaldi on an unpleasant errand
from Captain Sheridan. In a light-hearted reminder
of their old friendship, Garibaldi hands over his
identicard and link. Then, with all seriousness,
refuses to give up his gun. Zack has to insist and, as
Garibaldi relinquishes his military-issue weapons,
the atmosphere sours between them.

Wade takes Garibaldi down to the Customs Area
to meet a contact from Mars who wants to be
unofficially slipped onto the station. Among the
Humans and aliens passing through, Garibaldi sees a
woman standing nervously waiting. 'Lise...' he says
softly, recognizing her instantly as the woman he
was going to marry.

Garibaldi tries to control the emotions whirling
inside of him as he looks at Lise standing in front of
him in his quarters. She explains that after a messy
divorce from her first husband, she married William
Edgars, a powerful businessman on Mars. 'This is
the third time you've broken my heart, Lise,' he tells
her. 'That's one more than you're entitled to.' At
that, Garibaldi's door bleeps and Wade enters.
Garibaldi turns to the business in hand, wiping any
remnants of feeling from his face.

Zack breezes into his office and asks the computer
for a status report. Among the list of routine
security matters, it reports Garibaldi's unauthorized
entry into the Customers' Bay. Zack realizes he
deceived him and that he has a duplicate identicard.
Zack orders the computer to cancel all Garibaldi's
security clearances.

A man approaches Garibaldi, Lise and Wade and sits at their table in the bar in Down-Below. He hands over a vial encased in a molecular isoblock that can only be opened with a molecular code. Garibaldi looks beyond Lise at some men entering the bar as she explains the vial contains the cure for a viral plague that may threaten all telepaths. The men are beginning to worry Garibaldi and he suggests they leave. Before they get to the door, one pulls a PPG and points it at Lise. Garibaldi yanks her out of the way as the shot zooms past her. He punches one of the men, grabs his gun and the three of them scurry into the corridor.

Garibaldi taps frustratedly on the controls of a locked door until it is obvious his security clearance has been cancelled. He aims the PPG at the ceiling, shooting out one of the panels, and the three of them scramble into the overhead heating duct. Urging the others on, Garibaldi hangs back, ready to challenge their pursuers. A man's head appears through the opening and pauses as if listening to something. Garibaldi suddenly realizes what's going on and heads after Lise and Wade.

'Back away! Now!' cries Garibaldi. Lise and Wade scramble backwards through the duct as PPG blasts break through the floor from below. They make it to the ducts above a different room and Garibaldi tells them they are heading towards Docking Bay 3. Eventually, they reach another ceiling panel and drop down into a corridor. It is not Docking Bay 3; that is where their pursuers will have headed after picking up telepathically on their thoughts. Garibaldi grabs a passing security guard and tells him to get a team down there. Garibaldi follows on and finds Zack and his guards standing over the two telepaths who committed suicide as *soon as the security team arrived.*

Garibaldi returns to his quarters to find there is a message waiting from Lise. He considers for a moment, then tells the computer to delete the message without even seeing it. 'No,' he says to himself. 'That's all over.'

Garibaldi lies at the centre of the 'Conflicts of Interest' in this episode. The conflict is inside of him when Lise returns, dredging up memories which he dare not face because of the pain it has caused him in the past, and the fact that she is married to his employer. He acts against the interest of station security when he attempts to smuggle packages through customs. He no longer holds the privileges of authority, but he behaves as if he should have them, widening the rift between him and Sheridan and bringing him into conflict with Zack.

When Zack approaches Garibaldi on the orders of the Captain, there is a sense of a torn loyalty between them. Zack is reluctant to take Garibaldi's identicard and PPG, still hoping that he will come back to his old job. It is a difficult thing for him to do as a friend, but he pushes all those concerns aside to do his duty. 'In the end, we all have to take care of ourselves,' says actor Jeff Conaway. 'I don't necessarily want Garibaldi's job, but I've got it now and if I don't carry out my orders, somebody else is going to have to do it. So it's a point of growth for Zack, to be able to separate the two and carry on, no matter how painful it may be for him. It's a thing he's got to do because, in the end, loyalty really has to end up going to your commanding officer and since Garibaldi is no longer in that chain of command, I've got to be true to my school.'

This resolves any personal sense of disloyalty for Garibaldi. He no longer has any qualms about going up against the security team that he trained and nurtured.

He has severed ties with Sheridan, as he demonstrated when he agreed to team up with Wade, and if there were any doubt that there might be some lingering friendship or respect between them, it is dashed with Garibaldi's unapologetic defence of his actions to the Captain. The impression that emerges is of a hardened man who has closed off the attachments to his old life without replacing them with anything. But in the same episode, Garibaldi reunites a family separated from each other during the Shadow conflict, and that hardened man is counterbalanced with a compassionate side. '[That's] to reinforce that he hasn't had his personality completely changed or removed,' says writer Joe Straczynski. 'Parts of him that were good before are still good now, it's just that parts of his personality have been skewed to one side. That does kind of keep the audience a little off guard too, to say, well where is he in all this? He's not a bad guy, but he's not acting like one of our good guys, so what the hell is going on here?'

It also helps to keep the audience sympathetic towards him, despite some of the other things he is doing. That can also be said of his relationship with Lise, the woman he met on Mars and ran away from when he came to Babylon 5. In 'A Voice in the Wilderness' he discovered she had married someone else. 'Setting up Lise back on Mars and that relationship was definitely something I wanted to pursue down the road,' explains Joe. 'This gave me the opportunity to do so. There's always been stuff developing on Mars that I would have to get into with the whole Psi Corps situation. You really need something that ties us into that location, in the same way that Sinclair tied us into Minbar and in the same way that Cartagia ties us into Centauri Prime. By having someone there that Garibaldi knew, it made my life a lot easier in terms of laying a lot of foundation very quickly.'

The minute we see Lise standing in the Customs Area

looking vulnerable and alone, the scene looks set for a reconciliation between these two and a possible romance. She even seems ready to accept that, feeling a need to explain to Garibaldi what happened to her, opening a door for some kind of relationship, even though she is married. Garibaldi has that opportunity placed before him, but rejects it and frustrates the audience's expectations. 'He had to, to set up the complications of the character,' believes Jerry Doyle, who plays Garibaldi. 'You've got the one thing in life you should probably take the most care of, and pay the most attention to, and it's a life choice. It's one of those moments in your life maybe you look back on and say "God, what a mistake that was" She's a very nice girl, fun to work with, a knock out and so, for my character, not a bad day to go to work!'

Garibaldi is able to hide behind the job and avoid the issue through the work. Lise seems overly concerned about him when they are pursued by telepaths, but Garibaldi is only worried about getting them all through it. Chasing down a labyrinth of heating ducts could be considered a cliché, but it is given a freshness and a dramatic edge when those in pursuit fire through the floor. It was an effect achieved using a combination of computer graphics and on-set pyrotechnics. 'That was a potentially dangerous situation because if any of them had heads or faces above any of those hits at the time that they went off, then somebody could have been hurt,' says David Eagle who directed this episode. 'I made it very clear because of my experience on 404 [the explosion of Kosh's head in 'Falling Towards Apotheosis'] that there wouldn't be any mistakes. They took that very personally and made sure that nothing went wrong – and nothing went wrong. It went perfectly, that whole scene of crawling around in those air ducts worked very effectively, I think. The art department came up with a great design and the camera crews just did a great job.'

Another interesting scene from the filming point of view is Ivanova's trip to Epsilon 3 to arrange for some extra power to broadcast the Voice of the Resistance. She is surprised to find Zathras there, who turns out to be one of Zathras's nine identical brothers! 'I loved that,' says Claudia Christian, who plays Ivanova. 'That was like Bob Hope and Bing Crosby time, that was great. We did it in just one shot, there were no cuts. I love him [Tim Choate] the guy who plays Zathras, he's so fantastic. When people ask me if I would like to play any other character on *Babylon 5*, I always say it would be Zathras because it's such a great character.'

It is rare to do any scene in just one shot in television, especially one of this length. *Babylon 5* likes to be unconventional and so the decision was made in pre-production to film it in this way. 'I remember reading it and thinking, "gee, this kind of plays like Abbott and Costello's *Who's on First?*"' says David Eagle. 'I don't know whether it was Joe who said to me "David, I'd love to see this done in one take", or whether it was me who said "Joe, could I do it in one take?" All I know is that we were in absolute agreement. That kind of thing hadn't been done in a long time and this was a perfect opportunity to do a scene like this, four and a half pages long, in one shot, without doing any covers. I called the actors late that day – which was a week or so before we were going to film that scene – and I said "this is what I would like to do, will this work for you guys?" and they said "oh that's great, we'd love to do that!" I said "come in ready to do theatre, make sure you know those lines inside and out and are prepared to do the scene from beginning to end without stopping". They loved that idea, both Claudia and Tim. Tim said to me "wow, in twenty years of acting, no television director has ever called me up and given me more than a day's notice on how he plans to shoot something like this, I really appreciate it, thank you very much!"'

It was a technically complicated scene because the steadicam operator had to co-ordinate with the actors and so they performed it a total of seventeen times. But it was the second take that was the best and that was the one they used in the episode.

13:
'Rumors, Bargains and Lies'

Delenn calls Neroon to the White Star *as she heads towards Minbar. Although both risk alienation from their own castes for meeting, she appeals to him to help stop the civil war that has erupted on their home planet.*

Members of the religious caste gather on the White Star, *afraid that Delenn is planning to surrender to the warrior caste. Striking openly against her would tear their caste apart, so they decide to poison the ship with a residue siphoned from the fuel system and become martyrs to their cause. 'History won't even remember us,' says one, as Lennier listens unseen from behind. 'They will only wonder what happened to this ship and why it never reached home.'*

Sheridan is milling around the War Room as Ivanova is preparing to go on air as the Voice of the Resistance. He's excited about a new plan he has hatched up and wants her to mention that nothing happened today in sector 83 by 9 by 12. Ivanova protests that C&C reports say the area's quiet. 'So you can relax,' says Sheridan smugly, 'because what you're saying is absolutely true.'

A group of alien ambassadors watch Ivanova's broadcast with increasing unease. It has been a strange few days. White Stars have been involved in some secret attack, there has been an unexpected request for alien blood supplies from Franklin, and now there are suggestions of something happening in

Sector 83. 'They could be anywhere,' says the
Brakiri ambassador in panic. 'They could be all
around us!'

Faces of the religious caste conspirators cloud
over as Delenn tells them her plan is not to
surrender as they thought. It is too late to stop the
poison and their deaths, it seems, will be for
nothing. But Lennier is already climbing through the
air ducts, struggling to stop the poison before it
engulfs them all. He struggles to turn off the valve
as the canister bellows gas over him, then he
staggers back out into the corridor.

Later, as he recovers from the effects of the
poison that almost killed him, he tells Delenn it was
not sabotage. He explains to the conspirators after
she has gone that he did not want to destroy her
faith in the strength and wisdom of their caste. 'In
her world, we are better than we are... I much prefer
her world to my own and I won't allow anything to
threaten that.'

The League of Non-Aligned worlds has demanded
a meeting with Sheridan, angry at his constant
denials that something is going on. The ambassadors
demand the White Star fleet be put on patrol around
their borders. Sheridan refuses because they will not
give authorization to intercept passing ships. They
retaliate by saying they will, and that their ships will
join with the White Stars to show support for any
larger missions. Sheridan sighs resignedly, and
concedes to their demands. He walks out of the
council chamber and into the transport tube. The
doors close and he gives a triumphant 'Yes!' that
resounds up the corridor – he has got the Alliance
back together again and the alien worlds think it
was all their own idea.

Lennier's sleep is disturbed by movement outside

his room. He staggers to his feet and sees Neroon
sneaking out into his private flyer. Once on course,
away from Delenn and the others, Neroon sends a
message to the leader of the warrior caste. 'The
mission has been successful,' he says. 'I have access
to their plans to counter-attack our forces... Victory
will be ours within the week.'

Delenn's return to Minbar to deal with the civil war that is threatening to destroy her world has strong resonances with Mira Furlan's real life. She was a successful actress in Yugoslavia when hatred between the Serbs, Croats and Muslims turned to civil war. It was a war she was opposed to and, although born in what has now become Croatia, she felt no loyalty to any particular creed, and is in fact married to a Serb, director Goran Gajic. Therefore, Delenn's mission to end the fighting and bring peace to her world is something she can relate to. 'Absolutely, it's so well written,' she says. 'It's absolute reality from my experience. In times of war, all the people who support peace and talk about peace are hated by their own because it just can't be accepted. The war trumpet's sound is so loud that nothing else can reach people's ears and you're immediately accused of being a traitor if you pronounce the word peace. Then the war ends and everybody's taking photographs together, smiling and kissing and that's a weird situation because you – let's say, the pacifist – can't join them anymore because you remember. People have a very short memory and they get engulfed in this passionate hatred so they can't see the future and that they will get over it. So it's a very important episode, I think.'

Is that something she draws on when playing Delenn, or is it more Delenn's motives and Delenn's situation? 'Delenn is me, I am Delenn. It's all connected, it's the world we live in. *Babylon 5* is a metaphor for our life, our world, human relationships, for human behaviour, in peace, war, love, hate, death and so on. Of course, it's a part of who I am, all my thoughts are a part of what I am and what I play.'

That was very much the case with the scene of Delenn looking out across the destroyed Minbari city, remembering its former splendour, how her father used to take her there as a child and the destruction the war has wrought upon it. 'That was completely... I mean, I saw Sarajevo. Although I wasn't born there, I saw that city in my mind and the streets where I worked and where I lived. I shot a lot of stuff there, I really worked a lot in Sarajevo. I loved that scene, I loved that monologue. It's so poetic, and it's not in any way preaching, it's just images that you have that are heart-breaking because nothing is there anymore.'

This is not the first time that parallels can be drawn between *Babylon 5* and Mira's background and the conflict in the former Yugoslavia. She has said in the past that the Narn and the Centauri could almost be Croats, Muslims or Serbs fighting each other because of ancient feuds. But it is here where the comparison is most striking, something that Joe Straczynski is aware of and uses to his advantage. 'I'm not averse to using that in terms of the political context her character walks into,' says the writer. 'I know that if I start talking about differences in political groups fighting each other or ethnicity or what have you, leading into conflict and loss and life, when I put those words into her mouth they will come out again with the ring of truth about them. I suppose it can be considered a form of manipulation, but I'm comfortable about that. So yeah, I use it in so far as it doesn't conflict with the intent of what I'm doing with the story. I wouldn't use that background or nod in that direction if what was coming out wasn't right for the story.'

There is a determination in Delenn and a faith that she

is doing the right thing for all her people. It is what makes her approach Neroon, even though this may bring disapproval and suspicion from other members of her caste, and it is also what makes her blind to some of the realities about her people. Lennier seeks to protect her from these realities, deciding against telling her about the religious caste crew's plan to destroy their ship. He says that she does not walk in the same world that they do, and that he will not threaten her belief in the their caste by telling the truth. This is the depth of Lennier's loyalty, to put himself at risk to save her life and her cause, but to say nothing about it. 'He saves the day a lot and doesn't receive credit for doing it very often,' laments actor Bill Mumy. 'He's quite an efficient little guy in his own way. I enjoyed that episode a lot, it was a nice moment. I like it when Lennier's the hero and he effects something positive. There was a scene in that where I had to climb up this little vent. We did it at about eight o'clock at night and I'd been there since about four o'clock in the morning, and we did it over and over again because when you got to the top of this thing, they had a lot of trouble getting the smoke to come out of this little canister that was supposed to spew this poison gas thing out. So I had to go scaling, climbing up this hot little tube. It's like you're a sperm going through the ether or something. Did you ever see *Everything You Ever Needed to Know About Sex...*, the Woody Allen movie? I felt like one of those sperms, climbing through the tube. I'd get to the top and it didn't work and I had to climb back down again. We did that many times. People don't realize how many times we have to do these things sometimes.'

These events are balanced by a little levity on Babylon 5. Sheridan has got a little scheme brewing in his head and the very idea of it makes him giggle. 'He [Joe Straczynski] wanted that to be totally silly,' recalls Bruce Boxleitner. 'I said "this is way over the top", but he said he has to be absolutely off the wall because these people have to look at him and go "what's he smoking?" It's a light, strange side of him. When we look at the big picture of it, you've got to somehow like these people a little bit, even if they're a little quirky and goofy [because otherwise] when you get on to the dark stuff you're not pulling for them so much.'

The plan that Sheridan finds so amusing is designed to get the ambassadors from other races to agree to allow the White Star fleet to protect their borders. It is a move that will help them, but he knows they will be distrustful of it unless they think it is their idea. The way he achieves this is manipulative and dishonest, but it gets the job done. 'The whole Z'ha'dum thing was a transformational experience for him and there's many ways of showing that,' says Joe. 'If you look at Zen literature when somebody goes through a transformational experience, they often acquire a sense of humour in the process, you often have the laughing Buddha referred to in Zen. The other thing I wanted to do is show that he's learned a few things along the way. In the larger part of his career before this, he worked by basically banging his head up against the wall until the wall gave out. He's learned from Londo and others that there might be an easier way of doing these things, by being a little more manipulative, but also at the same time getting whatever he wants done without having to scream and shout all the time.'

At the same time, another one of Sheridan's little plans that he got all excited about is coming to fruition. The Voice of the Resistance is up and running, with Ivanova as the newsreader. 'That's exactly what it is,' says Claudia Christian. 'That's how they wanted me to do it, like a newscaster. I felt like Dan Rather or Walter Cronkite, the American newscasters. I was reading it from a teleprompter, they wanted that feeling, otherwise they would have made me memorize it. I memorized some of them, but I used a teleprompter for the rest.'

With everything apparently going well, striking back against ISN's propaganda, the White Star fleet patrolling to prevent attacks by allies of the Shadows and Delenn's peace crusade surviving an assassination attempt, it is the perfect time to throw a spanner in the works. Neroon sneaks off the *White Star* while most of the crew is asleep and it seems he is about to betray Delenn, setting up expectation for the next episode, 'Moments of Transition'.

14:
'Moments of
Transition'

Fire and smoke bellows from the buildings in the once-beautiful Minbari capital city. Delenn walks through the central temple, past wounded religious caste sheltering from the bombardment. Sadly, she looks to Lennier. 'Tell the warrior caste that we are prepared to surrender.'

Bester approaches Lyta as she sits quietly eating at the Eclipse Café. He knows she has been refused work because she is not a member of Psi Corps and he has a proposition for her. He'll slip her name off the rogue list if she agrees to leave her body to the Psi Corps after her death so he can discover how her abilities were enhanced by the Vorlons. 'I'd sooner put a bullet through my brain,' she retorts and storms off.

Lyta, now getting desperate for money, approaches Garibaldi for work. He doesn't trust telepaths, but he likes the idea of annoying Bester and a telepath could help him smuggle packages through customs for his new client, William Edgars. He agrees just as Bester passes by and Lyta reacts in shock. 'He scanned you,' she tells Garibaldi who runs after Bester and slams him up against the wall. Security guards pull him away, struggling, as Bester looks on with a smile.

Delenn, watched by the whole of Minbar, steps into the inner sanctum of the ancient temple where the leaders of the warrior caste are waiting for her. They plan to rule, but Delenn tells them that if they want to return to the ancient ways, the war must be ended by entering the Starfire Wheel. Whoever is prepared to die will win dominance for their caste. A rumble spreads across the temple and an iris opens above them. A beam of burning white light radiates down and Delenn steps into the circle. 'Shakiri,' she calls to the leader of the warrior caste. 'If you believe so much in your caste, enter the circle and die for them.' Shakiri protests, but after encouragement from Neroon, steps into the circle.

'We can walk out together,' Shakiri whispers to Delenn. 'Share the power.' She refuses and the Starfire Wheel increases in intensity. Shakiri feels himself burn, senses his approaching death and dives out of the circle. Delenn stays in and raises her arms up to embrace its immense power.

Neroon is aghast. 'When she proposed this, Delenn told me she would leave the circle after he did.' He watches as the circle continues to consume her body and she sinks to the ground. 'No!' he cries and rushes forward, lifting her out of the burning light. He is left standing in the Starfire Wheel, its intensity almost overwhelming, engulfing him in searing pain. 'I was born warrior caste,' he announces to the masses. 'I see now, the calling of my heart is religious.' The circle reaches maximum strength and, with a final bolt of incredible power, Neroon is vaporized.

Tears form in Lyta's eyes as she looks in the mirror at the Psi Corps symbol on her chest and the gloves on her hands. She was forced to accept Bester's offer when her job was taken away on Edgars' orders. 'By provoking Mr Garibaldi, I've put him... further on the path I need him to follow,' Bester records in his personal log. 'What I came here to get, I got. Even her.'

Delenn, barely able to walk after her ordeal, enters the Grey Council Chamber to summon the Nine who will lead her people. She calls five from the worker caste to dominate the warriors and the religious caste. 'They do not wish to conquer, or convert, only to build the future,' she explains. 'Judge wisely and well.'

The ancient temple that contains the Starfire Wheel was described as a vast, grand building. 'As big as a football field,' says the script, 'several storeys high, dome-like. Each storey rings the dome and, from behind smoked-glass windows, we see the silhouette of thousands of Minbari watching silently.' It was a difficult vision to achieve on screen. 'Almost impossible,' says director Tony Dow.

Most of it was achieved by shooting actors against a blue screen to enable a background to be added afterwards. One idea to give the temple more depth was to have sweeping panning shots which would require the background to change perspective in relation to the characters as the camera moved. This is usually achieved through a precise and time-consuming procedure known as motion control, whereby a computer records the camera's movements which can then be matched by the background matt painting. It was decided on this occasion to try a quicker method of putting targets on the blue background which the matt painter would use to track the changing perspective. 'The shots would really have been spectacular if in fact she [Delenn] had moved and we'd have been able to make a big pan across the background,' says Tony. 'It kind of worked out a little differently. When you look at those shots, they're truly difficult to do, and they weren't as impressive as they should have been for the amount of energy they took.'

The scene takes up almost a quarter of the episode

and Tony felt an essential part of increasing the tension through the scene was to show the Starfire Wheel getting more dangerous by growing bigger as Delenn stood inside it. 'The problem was, with the ceilings the height that they are, we couldn't put a light up there to shine down. So we had to hang a mirror and put the light on an angle off to the side and shoot the light into the mirror and have it reflect down. The problem was that we couldn't get a mirror that was really big enough to get the ring of light big enough so we couldn't really expand it. I couldn't get it to grow like it was supposed to. I mean it did grow, once I'd pencilled in the five stages of getting bigger, but at the end it was a little cramped, I thought.'

If Delenn showed her wholehearted commitment to peace in 'Rumors, Bargains and Lies', it is doubly so here. She is prepared to sacrifice herself for her cause, and even when the leader of the warrior caste has shown himself to be afraid and unworthy to govern, she does not turn back from death, but embraces it. 'She's Joan of Arc,' says Mira Furlan. 'Someone said to me today, do I see parallels between Delenn and Antigone? And, yeah, she's the heroine. I love playing that. She's the hero who has to die in order to prove his or her point and you just go to the end. That's the description of the hero in Greek tragedy. But Joe, because it's American television, he always saves her at the end, she always survives – I'm glad that she does because I still have a job!'

In terms of the story, it is Neroon who is her saviour. He pulls her from the Starfire Wheel because she is too precious to be sacrificed in that way, she still has work to do for Minbar. He is the one who becomes the martyr, taking her place and declaring himself to be religious caste at heart. 'It's a pacifist matter,' suggests Mira. 'You can be whatever you want to be. What you're born into doesn't define you. It's a very wonderful message with which I completely agree. It's like being a Serb or a

Croat. I actually know people who have become the worst nationalists, but for the other side, just for opportunistic reasons. Like a Serb who becomes the leading Croatian nationalist. Humans are Humans and they can be stupid and opportunist no matter what they are.'

Delenn's final action, having claimed victory for the religious caste, is to give away her right to rule. The Grey Council changes from a body of equal voices from the three castes to being dominated by the workers. 'We really hadn't seen much of the worker caste over the course of the four years, these are the guys who carry the bulk of the work of maintaining society and I figured it's their time to step into the sunshine a little bit,' says Joe Straczynski. 'It's also a way of saying that what you have here are two castes which are driving the boat, but have forgotten why they're driving the boat. I figured it was time somebody said "you've forgotten what the point of all this is". The Grey Council was formed as a barrier, or a form of defence, against the Shadows and when that threat was gone they needed to redefine themselves. They had defined themselves in that context for so long that they had lost the point of it. In a way it's a parallel to the Shadow War itself where you have these two sides who are carrying on their own agenda through a third party, which would be us. With Minbar, in trying to be prepared for combat, it had become its own worst enemy. The warrior and religious castes are like the Shadows and the Vorlons, with the worker caste caught in the middle. As we told those other two sides to go away because we're going to make our own way, the Grey Council had to take a similar direction.'

A more frivolous event is happening back on Babylon 5 with a certain Mr Adams trying to hire Garibaldi to find his dog and cat. This seems an unusual request until you realize that this is in fact Scott Adams, a cartoonist famous for his *Dilbert* comic strip which features the characters Dogbert and Catbert. He was invited to make a cameo appearance on *Babylon 5* after he wrote in *TV Guide* that it was 'the best show ever made'. 'It was a media zoo,' says Tony Dow. 'There were five or six different film crews and various different reporters. I realized that that's an important promotional thing for the show so you can't rush through that too much. We spent about twice as much time on that little section as we normally would have. It was fun to do.'

All this is an aside to the meat of events on Babylon 5 with the return of Psi Cop Bester. If the audience hadn't picked up the clues already, he confirms, through his personal log entry, that he was the one who programmed Garibaldi. The principle reason for his visit is to push Garibaldi further along the path he wants him to follow. The secondary reason is Lyta Alexander.

Bester wants her to rejoin the Psi Corps and approaches her in the Eclipse Café with an offer to do so in name only. 'That was the most fun both of us had had with our characters,' says actress Patricia Tallman. 'He was hysterical, I thought he was very funny in that scene, with the line "I want your body... no, no, no only after you're done with it". It was a chance for Lyta to tell him to go take a hike, and she's still much on top of her game, she doesn't think she's lost yet, she doesn't know, she still thinks she's got some options. She's in a mood, as I call it when I'm back in the States. It's one of my lines, I always say "I'm having a mood". She's been turned down for a job because she's not Psi Corps, but she's not given up, she's still got some ideas, you know what I mean? I like that about this character, but then it all gets thrown to the wind, she thinks she's got something with Garibaldi and then he tosses her out.'

By the end of the episode, Lyta is blackmailed into accepting Bester's offer, but it is just as much through the actions of the others on the station as it is in response to pressure from the Psi Cop. The depth of emotion at what it means to turn back to the organization that she ran away from is conveyed in one simple image. Lyta stands looking at herself in the mirror wearing the Psi Corps symbol and the regulation gloves with tears running down her face. 'The make-up girl came up with menthol crystals in a tube and you blow through it and that will make your eyes water. They said "she's going to need help crying" and I said, "go away!" It wasn't a problem to get to that point, I just had to stay in it.'

It is a moment of transition for her, joining Garibaldi's transition encouraged by Bester, and the transition of the Grey Council and Minbari society.

15:
'No Surrender, No Retreat'

'Enough is enough,' says Sheridan in his personal
log. The latest casualties in President Clark's
campaign were ten thousand civilians whose ships
were destroyed as they fled the killing zone. He has
decided the time has come to take back Proxima 3,
Mars and then Earth itself.

Londo timidly enters G'Kar's quarters. Their
meeting was pre-arranged, but G'Kar pays little
attention to his former enemy as he writes in his
book. Londo has come to ask that the Narn
government sign a joint statement with the Centauri
to throw support behind Sheridan. To that end,
Londo offers G'Kar a drink, as G'Kar once did for
him before the war. G'Kar picks up the glass and
holds it for a moment, before pouring the contents
back into the bottle.

Sheridan and the White Star fleet enter the space
around Proxima 3 where Earth destroyers have the
planet under embargo. Sheridan opens a link to the
Earth Alliance ships, ordering them to stand down.
'Your attacks on civilian transports are illegal,' he
tells them. 'You may leave peacefully if that is your
choice, but we are prepared to use force if
necessary.' Earth Alliance ships advance on their
position as Sheridan hears a familiar voice over the
link, Captain 'Mackie' MacDougan. 'C'mon Mackie,
President Clark is out of control... what does your
conscience tell you?' But his question remains
unanswered as Earth starfuries open fire on the

White Stars.

Sheridan's forces move in and the space around Proxima 3 becomes a panorama of swooping ships and exchanges of fire. Three Earth ships withdraw, including the Vesta commanded by Captain MacDougan. White Stars engage the two remaining Earth destroyers, advancing on the Pollux as it pounds them with its pulse cannons. One White Star is hit and spins uncontrollably into the destroyer, exploding on impact and engulfing the Pollux in a fireball. Sheridan watches helplessly from the head of the fleet, thinking of the crew who have just lost their lives.

Only the Heracles remains. Its systems are damaged, fire rages on the bridge and it is hopelessly outnumbered, but Captain Hall refuses to surrender. He knows Clark will hold him responsible if the mission fails and does not believe Sheridan will fire on them. 'You don't know that!' cries his second in command. 'I won't let you endanger this ship because you're afraid to face the consequences of your actions.' She orders the others to remove Captain Hall from the bridge and signals their surrender to Sheridan.

Sheridan brings together the commanders of the Earth Alliance destroyers and asks them to sign on board. 'Our mandate is to defend Earth against all enemies,' he tells them. 'Clark has become that enemy. Your oath is to the Alliance and the people back home, not to any particular government.' The commanders exchange looks. They'll have to talk it over.

Londo sits forlornly in the Zocalo bar, staring at the drink in front of him. He vaguely notices someone moving to sit next to him. He looks up to see it is G'Kar. The bartender fixes him a drink and *he knocks it back. 'Issue the joint statement,' G'Kar tells Londo. 'I will sign my name... But not on the same page.'*

Sheridan greets Mackie aboard the bridge of the White Star. The Heracles has decided to retire from the field, another ship will stay to defend Proxima 3 from Clark's forces, while he and Captain Kawagawa have decided to sign on. Sheridan shakes his hand warmly. The next step is Mars.

Tensions between Earth and Babylon 5 surfaced from the moment Sinclair took control of the station. He was an unpopular choice, often clashing with the administration back home. When Sheridan took over, those tensions increased until the station was forced to split from Earth. But that was just a breathing space. The issues that caused the station to reject President Clark's authority were not forgotten. Rather, they gained momentum as Clark took a stranglehold on power and engaged the military to back him up.

The new push in the storyline was greeted with enthusiasm by Bruce Boxleitner. 'That's when it got interesting again to me,' he says. He had been playing Sheridan's lighter side for several episodes and now seized the chance to rediscover his hard edge. Sheridan's determination to pursue his case against Clark is expressed in that single phrase, 'enough is enough', as the episode opens. This is the Sheridan who returned from the dead with a new zeal, not the Sheridan who was reluctant to take the stand against his own people when Babylon 5 broke away from Earth.

The opposition to Clark is shared by many, Edgars among them. But these characters, although agreeing with Sheridan's motives, disagree with his actions. They suggest there is a more subtle, less confrontational way of getting rid of Clark, and that casts doubt on the morality of Sheridan's actions. 'This is the predicament,' says Joe Straczynski. 'If you listen to what Edgars says, in many ways he has a valid point, and Garibaldi has a valid point. This show isn't about blacks or whites, it's about greys and each side tends to have a rationale to support what it wants to do. I think it's important to present that in a legitimate fashion. And, quite frankly, there is a real question of what does a soldier do if he feels the policies of his government are wrong? Obviously, you can refuse to take a direct order and face the consequences for that, but where is the line where you turn passive resistance into active resistance? That's not an easy answer to come to and that's the problem I wanted to play here with this episode and this whole season.'

From the very opening shot, there is a sense of moving relentlessly towards conflict, not only because of the characters' actions, but also because of the constant movement of the camera. 'I felt that the whole script should never stop,' says director Mike Vejar. 'I felt it should be driven throughout, this sense of almost a snowball effect where you're just caught up in all of the elements that are leading us to this war. Once you get on the thing you can't really get off.'

Keeping the camera moving is one of Mike Vejar's trademarks, which perhaps explains why he is so often hired for episodes that involve battles on the *White Star*. A constantly shifting viewpoint inside the ship can help create tension for the audience, especially when most of the action is going on outside with the characters pretty much stuck at their consoles. 'The *White Star* set is a very difficult set to make interesting,' acknowledges Bruce Boxleitner. 'It's very challenging for everybody to make that thing move and make it interesting, so the camera is moved a lot, a lot of tracking shots, around the chair and things like that, just to make it interesting. Basically it's all out there, blue screen out the windows and so, acting-wise, it's very strange. I kept asking to get up and walk around, get up and be around things more, so now every director wants to move me and I now ask "please can I go and sit down again?"'

One interesting device used in 'No Surrender, No Retreat' is shooting through the transparent battle plan on the ship, which is seen as a blurred image in the fore-ground. 'That's actually a device that the director of photography contributed,' says Mike Vejar. 'I love it as an effect, but it wasn't anything I thought of, John Flinn did. I think it was really a great device to bring about a sense of action and movement and being part of the ship.'

In an unprecedented move, Londo persuades Centauri Prime to put its weight behind Sheridan. He asks G'Kar to sign up to his public declaration of support, believing that the united voice of two former enemies will have a greater effect than either one of them on their own. 'Season Four is again about putting things right,' says Peter Jurasik, who plays Londo. 'Here he is again trying to move to a higher level. Londo can only do those through the political arena, he makes some growth and gets higher minded, but again it's through Centauri Prime. Although, I don't know if he's at all redeemed as a person because he's given so much up.'

'G'Kar doesn't cut him any slack at all,' says actor Andreas Katsulas who plays G'Kar. 'He remembers when he offered him a drink for peace in the Zocalo [in 'The Coming of Shadows'] and then found out Londo had just given the orders for the slaughter of many Narns. He'll never forget that.'

That is just one of the undercurrents running through the scene between these two. The memory of G'Kar's torture at the hands of the Centauri is also very fresh and, for Londo, there is a nervousness about approach-ing an old enemy to ask for a favour. This is all played out in a scene much longer than television normally allows.

'It's a real treat, it's a move towards the joy that one gets in the theatre,' says Peter. 'You get to do a whole piece rather than doing it piecemeal or patchwork. There's nothing more wonderful than when they give you the stage, and it doesn't happen often in television.

'Background notes for that scene were that they had scheduled it for a whole afternoon right up to the wrap and that day started getting further and further behind,' he adds. 'It was the only thing we had to do and we were both thinking "oh no..." and we were kind of hoping it would roll over to the next day. But they thought "let's just shove it in at the end of the day", so we got to do this scene with the producer tapping his toe and looking at his watch.'

However, Mike Vejar doesn't feel it was filmed in too much of a rush, and it certainly doesn't appear that way in the finished episode. 'One of the nice things about working with both Peter and Andreas is they are so pre-pared and so much fun to work with, they can take any idea and more or less go with it,' he says. 'Working with the two of them in a big scene like that at the end of the day for a director is just a dream because you know when you get there it's going to be ninety percent there and you just have to worry about focusing the camera in the proper way. It's not intimidating for me to have some-thing like that at the end of the day, it may be for an actor, but not for me. Again, that is a scene where we utilized the moving camera quite a bit. If I remember the scene correctly, we had about two places where we had a direct, very close eyeline to the actors. In other words, the angles were a bit off and what I was trying to do was get the feeling that Peter's character was genuinely trying to make a gesture to come together, but G'Kar was in no way ready to give that up. That sense that we really never got eye contact, except for a couple of times, was important to that particular scene to show two characters that aren't communicating.'

Londo leaves that scene with his tail between legs, as it were. But his words have not left G'Kar unmoved. The sentiments that he expressed would, indeed, be a help to Sheridan, and later G'Kar seeks out Londo and agrees to co-sign his declaration of support. '"But not on the same page", I love it!', says Andreas. 'It has to be gradual and I'm glad Joe's doing that. It would be so hokey if G'Kar said "oh yes well, let's be friends".'

G'Kar eventually does share that drink with Londo, and this time both of them are committed to what it represents. It takes the two of them a step further down the road towards reconciliation.

16:
'The Exercise of Vital Powers'

'Mars,' Garibaldi considers as a tube car speeds him towards a meeting with William Edgars, 'I can't believe I'm back on Mars. Three times before this place almost killed me. I swore I'd never give it another chance to finish the job.'

Garibaldi gets to see Edgars at last in his spacious home on Mars. The wealthy industrialist confirms he wants to see Clark stopped, but Sheridan's military action is the wrong way. Garibaldi agrees. 'Unless Sheridan's stopped,' he says, 'he'll tear Earth apart.' He won't hand him over to Clark, but Edgars could intervene, destroy the Sheridan threat and put himself in the right position to overthrow the President from the inside.

Four men bundle Garibaldi into a darkened room. Garibaldi turns, his heart pounding, to see a telepath sitting watching him. Edgars' voice speaks from behind a two-way mirror, reassuring him that he is in no danger, that the telepath is there to make sure he is telling the truth. Edgars asks him what he thinks of telepaths. Garibaldi glances nervously at the woman. 'I don't trust them,' he says. Edgars wants to know if Garibaldi really has a way to secure the man they talked about. 'I do,' says Garibaldi. The telepath nods to confirm it. Then Edgars asks the question Garibaldi doesn't want to answer. Is he still in love with Lise? 'No. No, I'm not,' says Garibaldi. The telepath looks to the two-way mirror and shakes her head.

A telepath lies unconscious in Medlab, the Shadow implants still protruding from his skull. Franklin has tried everything, but he can't revive him without him going crazy and he can't remove the implants without in-built Shadow defence systems killing his patient. As he walks away, frustrated, Lyta – who has come in search of Zack – looks curiously at the telepath. As she stares, the patient's eyelids flutter and the sound of a Shadow ship screeches through her mind. Her eyes intensify and the man wakes, getting off the bed. Franklin turns back to see the two of them put their hands up to each other, reaching out through the glass. Then Lyta turns away, the link is broken and the telepath collapses.

Edgars tells Garibaldi a story about a threat greater than Clark. About telepaths taking over and running society for themselves. 'A society where ordinary Humans are considered second-class citizens and privacy is something you don't even risk dreaming about.' It's a society that could exist if Sheridan isn't stopped. If he launches military action, Clark will set the Psi Corps loose and that will undermine Edgar's behind-the-scenes manoeuvres to overthrow the presidency. 'We're going to change the world, Mr Garibaldi,' he says. 'I hope you'll work with me.'

Franklin is working with Lyta to find a way of reviving the frozen telepaths, but Sheridan's refusal to say why it is so important is making it difficult. Sheridan concedes, at last, to tell him. It leaves Franklin troubled, and he wonders if other people were right when they said Sheridan was changed when he came back from Z'ha'dum. 'The Sheridan I know could never have told me what this one just did,' Franklin tells Lyta. 'He's right. It's the only *way. I just wish to hell he was wrong.'*

Garibaldi returns to see Edgars, having made his decision. He's in all the way and he's prepared to bring down Sheridan. 'Mars,' he considers as he heads off to make the arrangement. 'Three times before this place almost killed me. And now I've finally finished the job... It has to be done. I hope he can see that someday.'

Sheridan's mission to oust Clark continues with the determination that he had shown ever since returning from Z'ha'dum. He takes an almost autocratic stance, giving orders without explanation and expecting them to be obeyed. This is a man with a mission. This is war. Franklin, who showed an unwavering faith towards Sheridan in his speech to the Martian resistance leaders in 'Lines of Communication' needs an explanation here to understand why the telepaths with Shadow implants are so important.

'I think Sheridan has forced him to go to places where he didn't want to go as a doctor,' says actor Richard Biggs. 'Especially this doctor, Doctor Franklin, never wanted to be in a position where he had to choose death over life, and in the past when confronted with that situation he has always chosen life. There hasn't really been someone in his life that would force him to say "OK, we go the death way". In "Believers" with Sinclair he deliberately disobeyed an order because he couldn't come to terms with allowing somebody to choose death over life. Sheridan, on the other hand, has got the doctor to a place where he does realize that he will have to sacrifice these thirty telepaths for thirty thousand people. He doesn't like it, but at the same time he does know that he's right. And that's where the anger comes from.'

It is Lyta who provides the answer to the impossible question that Franklin had been wrestling with; how to revive the telepaths without them either latching onto the computer systems or being destroyed by the Shadow implants. She makes contact with the telepath in Medlab by accident and they engage in an unspoken communication through the glass. 'The telepath I was working with had his eyes closed, and he had to count to know what I'm doing,' remembers actress Patricia Tallman. 'We both had to have the same beats in our head so he knew when I was doing something that he should open his eyes, and then at one point he turns to me and I'm reacting — it was tricky. But it was fun. It's a challenge for actors, and he was great, Kenneth [Cortland]. He was a great actor, he was very good, very emotional, he was "there", obviously trained. I enjoyed that because you get guest stars and they all have different techniques, so you never know if you're going to gel with somebody.'

'That was a very time-consuming sequence to do,' adds director John LaFia. 'Maintaining the tension, trying to make you feel that these two are connecting telepathically. Just a lot of push-ins. The cutting took a while on that, too, to get that right just between the two of them and then pulling you into that sensation. I can't think of a better way to convey that than to constantly move in on each character, getting closer and closer and closer.'

The work against Sheridan's crusade is centred on Mars where Garibaldi is in discussion with Edgars about putting an end to his war with Earth. It brings him back into contact with Lise and this time there is no escaping his feelings. When Lise enters his room with a tray of food, she stands in front of the door, intensifying the feeling that he is trapped alone with her, unable to run away again.

Jerry Doyle was ultimately unhappy with his performance in that scene. 'That's where a couple of extra days, and a couple of million dollars more, you get to play with it a little bit more,' says the actor, who plays

Garibaldi. 'There are certain things I think I should explore when I am doing a scene, and the way she did it took me in a direction I wasn't ready for, I guess is the word. There were a couple of areas that I wanted to get to that I didn't get the chance to explore. But I thought she hit all the beats on that, she had the bitchy whiny thing at the beginning and she had to pull away with the desperation, she had the resolution, and once again at the end of the scene, the girl who matters the most walks out the door.'

There is obviously still an attraction between them, and the confirmation that he loves her comes when Edgars scrutinizes Garibaldi's motives while a telepath monitors his thoughts. The turmoil that must be whirling around in his head is reflected in his pacing like a caged animal in the room, looking at his warped reflection in an uneven mirror. 'Some of it was shot from a bird's-eye view to give the sensation that you were looking down on him,' remembers director John LaFia. 'The room is very black so you can't really see the walls, so you're stripping away the real world. He is constantly pacing round, but there's nowhere for him to go because she's in his head and physically he's trapped in this room, so it was really to make him claustrophobic.'

The actor who played Edgars, Efrem Zimbalist Jr – who Jerry describes as, 'a wonderful man, a pleasure to work with, he's just a pro, a sweet man, a great voice and a good head of hair!' – was on the set reading his dialogue for the scene, even though he wasn't visible. Ironically, it turned into an opposite situation for Jerry Doyle. 'That scene, I remember, really pissed me off because we had a sound problem on that and I had to go into the booth and loop almost the entire scene. I think if you ask the sound department they'll pretty much agree that I was a real asshole when I looped that scene. I knew it pissed me off the moment I heard it, and then I really let it piss me off, I let it fester, so that when I got into the booth I could get back to where I was in the scene. Sometimes these guys in the booth will see you coming in and they're like "oh shit, here he comes, he is out of his mind today", and then later I will say "nothing personal, I was just trying to get to a certain space". I find that pretty distracting work, you're in a meat locker, you've got a set of cans on your head, the sound doesn't sound the same and you're not back there, you're not on the set, you're not with those people, it's not the day, you didn't have the six-hour run-up of the day with other scenes to get to a certain place, your energy levels are at different areas, the pacing of your dialogue, your intention, your inflection, all those things are off. I don't enjoy ADR at all.'

That final revelation that Garibaldi really is in love with Lise, even though he tries to deny it, keeps the audience sympathetic towards him. Even though his actions in other areas are reprehensible, this helps to keep his humanity alive.

'The one area that Bester really didn't touch was his relationship with Lise,' confirms Joe Straczynski. 'So when he is with her he is more truly himself because that is the area that wasn't affected'

Everything else about him has been tainted by Bester's programming by this point, but Jerry believes the essence of his character still remains. 'Everything you've seen is the real Garibaldi,' he says. 'We all have certain traits and characteristics and insecurities and when we get pushed or tired or stressed, they tend to become amplified. I would have to say that maybe the relationship with Lise is one of the stronger of Garibaldi's characteristics, the desire to have that stability and consistency. He's not politic, and he's not subtle, and he doesn't trust people in authority, and he thinks most people who seek authority are the least qualified to have it. So I think all the elements of the character that you've seen are him, and that's why playing the character has been so fun because he has so many different ways to go. The relationship problems, the recovering alcoholic, getting fired four or five times from major jobs, having co-workers leave, transfer, die. All that stuff lays into the fact that he's directionally a very torn character and still trying to figure out who he is and what he's all about and what matters most.'

Finally, Garibaldi agrees to bring Sheridan to Mars and deliver him into Edgars' hands. John LaFia remembers enhancing the moment with the movement of the camera. 'I did some strange shots of Garibaldi. They're very quick cuts where you see the world moving behind him when he agrees to do this thing, just to give a sense of his world changing around him.'

It is the last step in Garibaldi's turn from friend to betrayer. Now only the formalities remain.

17:
'The Face of The Enemy'

'They've got your Dad, John,' Garibaldi tells
Sheridan over the com system. 'If you don't
surrender, they'll kill him.' This is the news Sheridan
dreaded. Garibaldi says he knows some people who
can bust him out, but Sheridan has to meet them on
Mars, alone. Ivanova begs him not to go, but
Sheridan still has some trust in Garibaldi and he has
to go after his father.

Sheridan walks into the bar on Mars, sees
Garibaldi sitting at a table in the corner and joins
him. Sheridan asks what he has to do. 'You've
already done it,' says Garibaldi, grabbing his wrist
and slapping a tranquillizer pad on his skin.
Sheridan tries to pull away, but Garibaldi's grip is
strong. Then the drug begins to take effect and
everything slows down. Strobe lights flash,
background music thuds and a group of men emerge
from the crowd. Sheridan tries to fight them,
throwing punches against the force of the tranq
taking hold of his body. They come back at him –
each blow feeling like an eternity in Sheridan's
drowsy world – hitting him in the face and kicking
him in the stomach. Garibaldi does nothing, he just
sits steely-faced as they take him down.

Garibaldi goes to see Edgars, having delivered his
part of the bargain. Now he wants to know the
whole story. Edgars puts his hand on a computer
pad hidden in the wall and opens a panel to a secret
store of isoblocks like the one smuggled through

customs on Babylon 5. Lise said that it contained a possible cure to a telepath virus, but Edgars had not told her that the virus was one he developed, and is contained in half the isoblocks. 'It's insurance,' says Edgars, 'against the day when they to do to us what we have done to them: turn us into second-class citizens. If they try it, we simply withhold the antidote.'

Garibaldi sits in a Martian tube car, expressionless, as Bester walks in and takes the seat opposite him. 'I can feel you, you know,' Bester comments. 'Beating at the inside of your skull, screaming to get out.' He pulls Edgars' plans to spread the telepath virus from Garibaldi's mind, then unlocks the memories that had been hidden from him ever since he returned to Babylon 5 after his missing fortnight. The Shadows had hoped to alter him to work for them, but telepaths in their service managed to get him out and bring him to a Psi Corps facility on Mars. There, they programmed him to be more rebellious, more stubborn and more suspicious of Sheridan and the others. 'It worked even better than I could have imagined,' reflects the Psi Cop. 'I have what I need. My interest in you is over.' Bester walks out of the tube car and, in a series of flashes that burn realization through Garibaldi's mind like lightning, his freewill is restored. Garibaldi slams his head back against the side of car and lets out a helpless cry of rage, frustration, anger and pain.

Garibaldi runs back to Edgars' home to find the place ransacked and his employer laying dead on the floor. The isoblocks containing the telepath virus and antidote are gone, and so is Lise.

The ISN news anchor smiles into the camera as she announces President's Clark's declaration for a

*day of celebration. 'The capture of renegade
EarthForce captain John Sheridan signals that the
war of aggression against Earth is unravelling,' she
says. Meanwhile, in a darkened cell somewhere on
Mars, a bloody and beaten Sheridan struggles
against the shackles that bind his wrists.*

Nothing was the same between Sheridan and
Garibaldi after they returned to Babylon 5.
Garibaldi's distrust of his friend and commanding officer
created a tension that turned to conflict and split them
apart. It brought Garibaldi to a point where he felt he had
to turn his back on Babylon 5, but when he left, he took
all those unresolved issues with him. Those issues continued to fester and, manipulated by his Psi Corps programming, he finally hands Sheridan to Clark. This final
act is a betrayal of everything he once fought for and,
moreover, a betrayal of a friend. With so much at stake,
so much history between them and so much emotional
charge built up over the season, it was imperative that
Garibaldi betray Sheridan to his face. 'You want to have
that dynamic of him sitting there passively as Sheridan's
getting the crap kicked out of him otherwise it loses half
its power,' says Joe Straczynski. 'Also from a story point
of view and a logic point of view, Sheridan wouldn't trust
anybody else. On some level, even though they've had
problems, he still trusts Garibaldi, because they've had
four years together. If it was anybody else, a third party,
he would have brought a lot of back-up with him.'

As it is, Sheridan leaves himself wide open and pays a
harsh penalty. He is drugged and outnumbered, but he
still puts up a desperate fight in a scene where all the
emotions are displayed. 'We shot it along with the song,'
remembers Bruce Boxleitner, who plays Sheridan. 'He
[director Mike Vejar] brought in a tape, he just saw this
as a song and it was a really intense thing, it was a slow

build up until the drug hit and then it was really heavy metal. We did it all with strobes and still shots. I thought that was an interesting thing, using stills interspersed with the speed of the thing, jarring and violent, but you never really see blood and stuff like that, just suggested violence.'

'In my mind I saw it pretty much the way I did it with the strobing lights and the added element of being tranquillized,' says Mike Vejar. 'I tried to go from the strobe lights as something that was just an effect in the background to something that suddenly took over and added to the drama of the event. We changed camera speeds from normal speed to high speed and then back again to try and get that druggy flavour, the feeling of what Sheridan was going through while he was being attacked. I think also in the script, the description I took really to heart was that it was really like a lion being taken down by a group of hyenas. Joe described it as not a bar fight, so I wanted to make the take-down when these guys subdued Sheridan not like a typical bar fight where he was punching people and everything, but one where he was just trying to get out of there and he was outnumbered and finally taken down.'

The stills interspersed in between the slow motion footage were not freeze frames, but were taken on set by a stills photographer. 'There was three places within the show where we utilized still cameras,' says Mike. 'We did it with Garibaldi's realization of what he had done on the tube car on Mars, on the fight sequence with Bruce and in the final scene where we get all the snippets of evidence at the murder site. When I read that last scene, I felt the crime scene utilizing still frames would be interesting there, and using it as a style for the other two scenes would be visually interesting.'

The expression on Garibaldi's face highlighted in the strobe lighting says everything about what he has done.

The perfect set up for that, according to Jerry Doyle, was the scene before which relates his actions to the betrayal of Jesus for thirty pieces of silver. 'You don't have to do much as an actor after you have a set-up line like that,' he says. 'Knowing how important my father was in my life before he died, to use Sheridan's father as the shield to take him down and betraying a friend, this is as the actor playing the character – no acting required. You've just got to think about that... I remember sitting there and watching it happen and you want to say "stop", you want to go kick the shit out of all the guys that are beating him up and you can't. I am thinking, what have I done? There's nothing I can do about it. I'm so disgusted with myself. Then to watch him land on the floor when the camera trucked in on me, I was just sitting there and I was almost dead, the person that I thought I was, the things that I thought I believed in, the friendships that I thought I had, if none of that was true, then I'm not really here. So I just tried to roll over the eyes of the shark and say inwardly to myself "I'm really in it now, I'm where I want to be, with who I want to be with [Edgars] and where I want to be with him" while saying at the same time "I've done something very, very wrong".'

Having done the wicked deed, Garibaldi makes contact with the person who conspired to manipulate his actions – Bester. It is the second big confrontation of the episode, and one that contrasts with the brutality of Sheridan's capture. This is no argument or fight with an exchange of hot-headed emotions, this is a quieter moment and it is all the more effective for that. 'It puts two characters into a situation where they're in a tightly enclosed space,' says Joe Straczynski. 'It increases the sense that Garibaldi's trapped, he's caught in something very small, very tight, he can't get out of it. He's helpless and that heightens the emotion of what he's going through. I wanted it to be in totally the opposite direction, emotionally, to go from the extreme of the huge event of Sheridan's take-down to a whisper. But it's a very cold, deadly whisper in a very tight space where there's no escape.'

'That, to me, is what hell like is,' comments Jerry Doyle. 'If there is a heaven and a hell, hell is the place you go after you watch the video of your life in front of all of your friends and family and they show you every missed step, everything you did wrong in life on this giant video in front of everyone.

'Walter [Koenig, Bester] did a wonderful job with that,' he adds. 'He had to talk his ass off all day long. He had really good transitions in there, he had evil, good, macabre, and the hardest thing was to sit there and not react to it. I was supposed to be some automaton. I also thought the camera crew did a great job with the scene they had to push in on my eye. It looks like an easy shot to the audience, but it is such an intricate shot. It was some special lens with this unbelievably complicated focus knob on it and they started on my eye and they back away because they're afraid that if they go the other way and go a little too far – ow! my eye! Then when they reversed the film I thought it was pretty dramatic. I remember how technical the scene was because it was such a tight space too, to get into Walter and reverses and set the strobe lights. That was all done by hand. We had guys sitting on the floor running flags through lights to simulate the strobe effect and the guys couldn't see each other on the other side of that shuttle car, so they had to time it. There was a lot of stuff going into that day to make it work.'

When Bester has finished his speech, he simply walks away leaving Garibaldi with the knowledge of what he has done and the only thing he can do is let out his anguish in a scream. 'Joe didn't write it out that "when this is revealed to you, you have to do this, this and this". It said

"Garibaldi reacts" – it leaves it pretty nebulous. I thought I can't encapsulate that moment when it's all laid out in front of me because there was so much going on. The only thing I could do was slam my head against the wall and let it go. That, to me, was the trumpet call to action. OK, now that I've found out what happened, you f**ked with me, now I've got some stuff to do' says Jerry Doyle.

18:
'Intersections in Real Time'

Sheridan lies on the floor in a darkened corner of the drab, grey cell where he has been incarcerated since his capture. The door opens and he stirs, squinting into the light from the corridor at a man standing in the doorway: his interrogator.

'When I ask you a question, you will respond at once,' says the interrogator with the routine of a man who has done this many times before and is comfortable with his work. 'Co-operation will be rewarded, resistance will be punished. Do you understand?' Sheridan goes after him, but after a few steps, metal bands around his neck and wrists spark with electricity and he staggers back in pain. 'Paingivers... If you come within five feet of me, they will hurt you. If you come within two feet, they will render you unconscious.'

Guards enter the cell, grab Sheridan and drag him fighting to a chair in the centre of the room. They hold his arms down as metal restraints clamp around his wrists and ankles. He stares at his interrogator who opens his briefcase and takes out a pen, notepad and a sandwich which he bites into with relish. 'Would you like some?' Sheridan looks at the sandwich longingly; he hasn't eaten in two days. The interrogator releases the shackles around his wrists and Sheridan grabs the food. Only after Sheridan has eaten it is he told the sandwich contained toxins.

Sheridan lies on the floor, shaking and sweating

after a night of fevered sickness. The interrogator enters and invites him to return to the chair. Summoning up his remaining dignity, Sheridan obeys and restraints clamp around his wrists and ankles again. Guards drag a Drazi into the cell and sit him down. He sobs as the interrogator sets up a recording device and tells him to relay the same confession he gave last night. Sheridan listens as the Drazi says he conspired with Sheridan, Ivanova and Delenn to overthrow the Earth government. Sheridan begs him not to do it. 'I don't know what they've done to you in here,' he says. 'But... it's all flesh... As long as you don't break inside, they can't win.' When the Drazi refuses to say anymore, he is taken away to be killed.

The interrogator pushes a piece of paper in front of Sheridan on which is typed his confession. All he has to do is sign it, make a public statement and then he can leave. 'Don't you want to be free to walk out that door, to feel the sun on your face again?' And Sheridan does, so much. He is almost ready to accept the interrogator's enticing words when he looks up and, though his exhaustion, sees the image of Delenn in front of him. The hallucination of her beautiful, unwavering form returns a flicker of determination to his eyes. From somewhere in his dry mouth, he finds some spittle and spits on the paper.

The interrogator gives him one last chance to confess or die. Sheridan refuses. He is strapped to a gurney and wheeled away. This is it, this is the end, the end of torture, the end of struggle, the end of pain. Sheridan lies back, resigned to death.

Guards rush in, pull him off the gurney and plant him a chair just like the one he left in the other room. Restraints clamp him into place and a new

interrogator walks in. 'Resistance will be punished,
co-operation will be rewarded,' he declares.
Sheridan hangs his head. His ordeal is beginning all
over again.

There was a great deal of excitement surrounding
'Intersections in Real Time' before it went into production because it was obvious Sheridan's torture
scenes were going to be some of the strongest
attempted in *Babylon 5*. Then disaster struck when the
actor who had been cast to play the interrogator,
'William', pulled out at the last minute. Earlier in the year
he had worked on a pilot film for Disney and suddenly
they wanted him back to re-shoot some scenes. Because
it was a prior contract that took precedence, there was
no way he could refuse.

Babylon 5's producers got straight on the phone and
called Raye Birk's agent. Raye had impressed them at
the audition and was their reserve choice for the role. He
was working on a sitcom called *Caroline in the City* when
he got a call to say he was wanted on *Babylon 5*. 'I said
"you're kidding!" Raye remembers. 'My agent said "no,
no, they want you to do it". I said "what happened?" He
said "don't ask!"'

It was already Tuesday afternoon and Raye was due on
set on Thursday, but he still had the sitcom to film. 'In
between working on these scenes for this situation
comedy, I would be trying to get the lines down for
Babylon,' he says. 'Wednesday was the shoot day for
this sitcom and I was there for eleven hours doing that,
trying to squeeze any extra time getting ready for
Thursday. I got over there Thursday morning and started
and we had a very bumpy day the first day, but I had a
lot of support from the team over there, the director,
Bruce Boxleitner, the producers, John Flinn who is the
director of photography. They couldn't have been more

supportive and helpful.'

'Had he not been as prepared as he was, it would have been harder,' says Bruce Boxleitner, who plays Sheridan. 'I thought he was marvellous as sort of this everyman type of man. He set up all those nice little things, the character was such a little prissy guy.'

Despite the last-minute rush, Raye Birk was soon able to find his feet with the character. The second day included scenes he had prepared for the audition, helping things go smoothly from then on. It was then suggested he could re-shoot some of the scenes originally shot on that first 'bumpy' day. 'At the end of the first day my energy and concentration really started to break and come apart and I had trouble sustaining the scenes,' he explains. 'We were doing it in little bits, chunks and pieces, not whole sequences, which is always unfortunate, but it's one of the ways of getting through. The next day went very well because it was material I was a little bit more familiar with and John Copeland, one of the producers, came down and said "I looked at the dailies, we can piece what you did yesterday together, it will look just fine, but if you finish up early enough on Tuesday" – Tuesday was the day I was due to finish – "we can re-shoot your close-ups". I was enormously grateful and, indeed, we did finish in time and we shot all the close-ups on single takes on Tuesday. I was very pleased with the way it came out. I think it's one of the most satisfying pieces of television I've done. It's a great role and a wonderful opportunity.'

Bruce also enjoyed himself tremendously on the episode. 'I loved it,' he says. 'It was just two characters, you don't get to do that too often. He did most of the talking, but nevertheless I had my own thing going. It doesn't lessen the job just because you're not doing all the talking. Listening, reacting or not reacting, resisting, being sick and feeling drugged. All those acting things were fun, you don't get to do that often. That's what's great on this show, we all get to do things that you don't normally get to do. It was the real final trial for Sheridan, time to do some juicy stuff, to be all grubby and sticky and I don't care.'

Bruce played Sheridan's torture scenes by imagining the soreness from having been beaten up in the previous episode, being drugged, weak and not eating for days – apart from the corned beef sandwich, of course. 'I ate four corned beef sandwiches – four of them!' he says 'And I ate them. A lot of times actors will have a bag to spit it out in, but I ate them. I've not had one since, either.'

The confrontation between Sheridan and his interrogator is quite intense, almost brutal, even though there is little actual violence. The experience of watching it can be quite shocking, especially when you realize that much of the episode is based on Joe Straczynski's research into real instances of torture. 'I had relatives who were on the run in the Second World War and I've followed a lot of these kinds of stories in the past. I also did one degree in clinical psychology and a second degree in sociology, part of which involves the study of how people brainwash and what the techniques are. I've studied cults and learned about brainwashing techniques there. I sort of lumped all this together and put it into the episode and tried to do it in a way that didn't say "I have a college education and you're going to pay for it"!'

This is not the first time torture has appeared in *Babylon 5*. The interrogator tells Sheridan the paingivers around his neck and wrists were bought from the Narn, referring back to the paingivers used on G'Kar in Season One's 'Parliament of Dreams'. There was also the memorable arrival of a Vorlon inquisitor in Season Two and Cartagia's treatment of G'Kar earlier in the season, making it somewhat of a recurring theme. 'I like to take characters and put them in jeopardy,' says Joe. 'I like to play with what happens to a person emotionally when you stick them up against the wall and the best way of doing that is to isolate them from everything else and make them helpless. The only way they can get out of it is if they pull upwards from there using the inner resources of their soul.'

Sheridan finds that inner strength to resist the appeals of his torturer, even though the temptation to end the suffering must have been great. At one point he seems almost ready to sign a confession, but from somewhere within himself he conjures up the image of Delenn and his strength returns. Bruce Boxleitner thought there could have been more moments like this. 'I played more scenes in this thing where I literally was breaking and Joe cut them out,' he says. 'He wanted me to be tough the whole way, but I wanted him after the sequence where they dragged the Drazi out, to be kind of losing it. I did one where I was almost raving and screaming, giving in as opposed to holding it together. I know he didn't use that one.'

'The reality is that not everyone does break,' says Joe. 'Fundamentally the show is about – and I've always said this about the series – the fact that hope exists in the darkest of rooms, it exists in the voice that says "I will not break and I will not bend". That he doesn't break is, to my mind, a statement that no matter how terrible the odds, no matter how alone we are, we can still persevere. If he were to break then it would send the other message that in the end the state will always win. No, you can fight the state and you can win and it isn't a win in terms of a victory over massive forces, it's a win over yourself.'

The original script included a lot of other material outside of the interrogation room, involving Garibaldi's attempt to convince the Mars resistance that he was programmed by Psi Cops. All this material was filmed, but ended up being cut from the episode. 'I'd always wanted to do a two-character, one-room episode and every time I came up to doing it I kind of chickened out at the last minute and put in some B-story stuff,' Joe explains. '"The Inquisitor" was that way, and "Convictions", and other stuff. I was going to do it in this one and I chickened out at the last minute and put the Garibaldi thread in. Then what happened was this episode came in about seven or eight minutes long and the next episode came in almost seven minutes short, which to my mind is the universe saying "do what you wanted to do in the first place". So we just took those scenes and shunted them over into the next episode and they blended in perfectly and it made the first one what it wanted to be in the first place.'

19:
'Between the Darkness and the Light'

Garibaldi sits in the tunnels controlled by the Mars resistance, branded a traitor. Number One aims a PPG at him and prepares to fire. 'No!' cries Franklin and dives at her. Her gun shoots at the ceiling as they both go down, wrestling for the PPG. Others rush forward and Lyta grabs at a rifle and fires it above their heads. They scatter and now she is in control of the situation. Garibaldi looks at Lyta, begging her to scan him and find out the truth. 'If you don't they're going to kill me,' he implores. She enters his mind and burrows deep. He shakes as the painful memories are pulled from him one after another until he screams with the trauma and she retreats. Then Lyta turns to Number One and sends the same images to her brain.

Garibaldi, Franklin and Lyta walk through miles of Martian tunnels and break into the military facility holding Sheridan. Lyta pulls the entry code to Sheridan's cell from the mind of one of the guards and they enter. Light from the corridor falls on Sheridan's abused body and the three of them stare, mortified. He looks half dead, pale and worn from the torture and drowsy from the drugs.

Franklin and Lyta virtually drag Sheridan out, following Garibaldi to the check point and the gateway to freedom. The guard behind the window regards them suspiciously, as do others who advance

*from behind. 'Step away from the prisoner,' orders
the guard. Garibaldi makes a break for it, pulling
his PPG and firing on him. Franklin throws a punch
at the guard behind, and they dive for cover as an
exchange of gunfire breaks out, setting alarms
blaring. Garibaldi yells to run, but the guard he shot
is still conscious and, unseen by him, raises his gun.
A PPG blast sails past Garibaldi and strikes the
guard down dead. Garibaldi looks back and sees
Sheridan, a mad determination burning in his eyes,
and a freshly used PPG in his hand.*

*White Stars arrive at the rendezvous point for the
resistance only to find an EarthForce fleet waiting
for them. The ships are covered in a Shadow-like jet
black and speckled skin. They order the resistance to
surrender, but Ivanova refuses. 'I am Death
Incarnate,' she says, 'the last living thing you're ever
going to see.' She fires the first shot and space erupts
into battle. White Stars and EarthForce fighters
dance round each other in a sea of energy blasts,
creating one fireball after another as destroyers and
White Stars explode. Ivanova, under protests from
Marcus, sets a collision course with one of the
destroyers, constantly firing at the Shadow-skinned
Earth vessel. It explodes just before they collide,
sending a massive bit of flaming debris spinning
towards the* White Star, *striking it with a crippling
blow.*

*Marcus struggles to pull Ivanova from the
wreckage of the White Star. He drags her out of the
door, through the fire and smoke and past the
bodies of the dead crew to a lifepod.*

*Sheridan joins the White Star fleet, the memory of
his interrogation still fresh in his mind. He finds his
way to one of the sickbays where he sees Marcus
sitting by Ivanova's side. 'We got them,' she tells*

him in a brief moment of consciousness. 'We cleared the way for you, John. All the way to Mars.' She reaches out her hand wearily and Sheridan takes it. 'I'm not going to make it, am I?' Sheridan looks back at her, and with sadness in his eyes, tells her she is dying.

Fate must have intervened when 'Between the Darkness and the Light' was being filmed, because when all the material was edited together, it came out several minutes too short. This was a godsend to the production because it enabled essential scenes cut from the previous episode to be slipped in seamlessly. The most significant of these is where Garibaldi pleads for his life.'That scene was especially frustrating,' says Richard Biggs who, as Franklin, was the one invited to pull the trigger. 'There were so many different ways I could have played it and we didn't have that much time. I remember Jerry, Pat, Marjorie [Monaghan, Number One] and I would get together and try to find the different angles, the different layers and try to give the audience "is he? isn't he? he is, no he's not" type of a thing moment to moment. Because on *Babylon 5* with Joe it could easily happen. It's not going to be one of those shows where you go, "you know he's not going to do it", *Babylon 5*'s not like that. So we wanted to take advantage of that and at each moment have the audience going "he isn't... he is... no, no, no!"'

The scene is a mass of split loyalties. Franklin and Lyta are revolted by the heinous crimes Garibaldi has committed, but they still remember the man he used to be. Could they seriously condemn him without giving him a chance to tell his side of the story? 'Gosh, I went through a lot of transitions with that,' says Patricia Tallman, who plays Lyta. 'At first I felt that I would be very sympathetic to him because he talked about being messed with by

Bester and I understand what all that's about. Then I thought, but he's betrayed Sheridan and Sheridan's a hero to me. So there was this conflict going on and I realized that's it. She is conflicted about this.'

The most powerful moment, though, belongs to Jerry Doyle, with Garibaldi's reaction to Lyta pulling the memories from his mind using a scan so deep it risks damaging him. On the day, most of the scene was filmed in the morning, leaving his close-ups until after lunch. 'After lunch, we call it post-lunch syndrome,' says Jerry. 'After a meal your energy levels dive and I try to take a little power nap during lunch. I kind of kept this little footprint of what was going on when we shot the last part of it before lunch and I went back and fortunately I got back there. I remember it was a pretty long scene, a lot of movement for some of the actors and cameras and we got it done and they go "cut", and the director goes, "damn!" Rick comes up and goes "man, you nailed it!. The director goes "do another one" and I said "I really don't think so", and he goes "you're right, f**k it, that was up!"'

'Jerry Doyle – he kills me, he's such a crack up,' says Patricia Tallman. 'Of course they start on me, I'm doing all my reactions on the master take and I know he's kind of hanging back, a lot of people don't go full out, I expect that. When they turn the camera round he did something very different, and I would have been different. I will be very interested to see how it cuts together because I don't know if it will make sense. Will it make Lyta look really harsh?'

The scenes of them breaking into Sheridan's cell that follow are part of the original script for this episode, but what Franklin does in one of the fights was certainly not. The script has Garibaldi gesturing to Lyta and Franklin to move ahead while he deals with two guards who are patrolling the tunnel. However, Rick Biggs thought it would be great if Franklin took part in the fight. 'I wanted to be involved in the saving of Sheridan,' he says. 'Joe had been painting my character as a hero for weeks now and I didn't want him to hide in the time of crisis.'

David Eagle, who directed the episode, was reluctant to agree. 'I said "Rick, it's not scripted this way and you know we generally stick very close to what Joe's script says, particularly in terms of something like this because it may have an effect on something that's going to happen in the future. This is not really my call." I thought that was the end of it, then Jerry Doyle and Pat chime in in support of Rick "oh come on Dave, let him get into the fight, he never gets into the fight". Then I see that the whole crew is waiting around watching this, wondering how I'm going to deal with this. It's like, how's Dave going to get out of this one? So I look at my watch and see that we've got five minutes before lunch, so I say "OK, let's break for lunch, and I will talk to Joe".'

Joe Straczynski wasn't there, so John Copeland gave the go ahead and Rick Biggs finished his lunch early to rehearse with the stunt co-ordinator. After lunch, everything went fine first time around. The problem came in the second take. 'My skills as a boxer left much to be desired as I split open the stunt man's eye!' Rick explains. 'So I don't tend to ask to get into the stunts any more, I leave it to someone else.'

'Rick is a very physically well-built guy, he exercises, he's very muscular, he's very strong,' says David Eagle. 'He just let this stuntman have it, he didn't mean to, but he decked him, he knocked him unconscious. There's blood all over the place, I thought the guy was going to lose his eye. I mean, it was a very serious injury. This poor stuntman had to go to hospital. Rick was just devastated by it, he was very upset. He didn't mean to do this and after making such a big deal about getting into the fight and causing such a ruckus and using up time to do that, here this happens. I said "don't worry about it, the guy will come back and if he's OK we'll bring him back to the set later and you'll apologize to him", and he said "look, I will never ask you or any other director to change anything ever again".

'In fact, when you look at it, you will see that shot. We had to use it because I only had four shots for the entire fight, the two shots I took before and the two shots we had on this take. Then we lost our stuntman. And you'll see when he decks him, the guy goes right out like a light and Rick goes down with him just to check him for a fraction of a second. He thought he went out of character, but he actually stays in character, it's almost like the concerned doctor, he knocks the guy out and bends down to see if the guy's OK.'

In the fictional world, it is Ivanova who is injured. Her action in the battle against the elite EarthForce ships was suicidal and the victory which she achieved was not without cost. Ivanova is dying and, at one point, this seemed like it would be the end of the character's life on *Babylon 5*. 'I actually considered for a while let's just maybe kill her,' reveals Joe Straczynski, 'but I figured that there's more that I can do with this character. Every season I spin the bottle and whoever the bottle points at gets it, and in a way that keeps me fresh.'

It gave actress Claudia Christian the chance to play a death scene. 'Yeah, that was great. It was very emotional and very sad, there were a lot of tears.'

Some actors use tricks such as glycerine to simulate tears, while others need to concentrate their emotions to get themselves to cry on screen. For Claudia, playing such an emotional scene is not a problem. 'In fact, I always joke to the director "do you want the tear to come out of the right eye or the left eye?" I mean, it's really not difficult for me. Not that I've had such a tragic life or anything, it's just easy for me to get the emotion out. It's also because the writing is good so when the situation is real, you can put yourself in that situation. It's easier to come up with the tears that way.'

At the end of the episode it really seems as if Ivanova might die. *Babylon 5* has not shirked from killing off or removing characters in the past and Franklin's medical diagnosis reveals there is no hope for her. But, on *Babylon 5*, there is always hope, and in science fiction, nothing is impossible.

20:
'Endgame'

Frozen telepaths in cryonic units pass by Franklin and Number One on their way to be smuggled into every one of the thirty EarthForce ships guarding Mars. Number One looks at the cargo suspiciously. 'I really hope you know what you're doing,' she says.

An explosion blows open the door to the defence bunker on Mars, and Garibaldi and Number One break in wearing breathing masks. The lack of oxygen from the invading Martian atmosphere claws at the lungs of the EarthForce personnel who are quickly disabled by the resistance.

A jump point forms at the edge of the Martian atmosphere and Marcus and Lennier bring the White Star 3 *swooping down across the surface, firing at parked shuttles and munitions dumps. A defence tower turns and targets them. It fires, but is cut short as Number One engages the weapons from the bunker and blasts the tower to pieces.*

Lyta stands on the Martian surface as the reflected light from the explosions dance across her face. She lifts her eyes to the sky and sends a telepathic signal to the telepaths in each of the thirty EarthForce destroyers above. The telepaths emerge from their cryo units, searching for the machine. Their minds find the ship's computer systems and latch on, crippling the ships from the inside. Jump points form around Mars and Sheridan's fleet emerges, striking at the engines and weapon systems of the destroyers, disabling them permanently.

As the fleet prepares to jump to Earth, Marcus

steals away from Lennier and links in to Babylon 5's medical files. Something Lennier said to him earlier has made him suspicious. Buried among Franklin's records he finds what he was hiding – there is an alien machine on Babylon 5 that can replenish someone's life by taking the life force from another.

Jump points open around Earth and Sheridan's fleet spills out. Captain Sheridan addresses his home planet from the command chair of the Agamemnon, 'We come on behalf of the thousands of civilians murdered under orders from the current administration... We are here to place President Clark under arrest, to disband Nightwatch and return our government to the hands of her people.' But in Clark's office on Earth, the President holds a PPG to his head and fires. On his desk is a simple two-word message, 'Scorched Earth'.

The orbital defence platforms surrounding Earth turn away from Sheridan's forces and back towards the planet. 'Captain, you have to stop them before they fire,' appeals Senator Crosby from Clark's office. Sheridan hits the com system and calls to Delenn and every ship in the fleet. Minbari destroyers stream out of Delenn's cruiser and swarm side by side with Earth destroyers, targeting the platforms. The Agamemnon is rocked by missiles coming in on all sides. Fire and smoke erupts on the bridge and its weapons systems are disabled. Sheridan watches as one of the defence platforms turns towards North America, building up energy ready to fire. A sudden calm descends over him. He realizes what he has to do and gives the order for ramming speed.

The engines of the Agamemnon flare to life and it speeds towards the platform. At the same time, a jump point opens and an Earth destroyer comes out *firing. The platform explodes and the* Agamemnon *plunges into the fireball... and out of the other side. The bridge is filled with the cries of victory.*

Back on Babylon 5, Marcus has found the alien machine and fitted it to Ivanova's dying body. 'I love you,' he tells her as it takes away his life to give to her.

When 'Endgame' was completed, Joe Straczynski predicted that it would be one of the fans' favourites of the fourth season. 'Because it does so much to resolve the Earth thread,' he says. 'It's just wall-to-wall action and wall-to-wall complications.'

The man chosen to direct this episode was Captain Action himself, producer John Copeland. 'Joe kind of hand-crafted this one for me,' he says. 'He told me "you'll do really good at this if it doesn't kill you" – those were his exact words to me when he handed me the script. When we edit together, when we do our cuts on the episodes, he refers to me as Captain Action and I most often take the lead in massaging the action sequences of the episodes and Joe takes the lead with the dramatic portions. I like to think that over the years in my student films and in the things that I've done since then, action is the thing I am really good at, so I think he gave me something that played to my strengths a little bit.'

There are space battles, ships falling apart, fire, smoke, people breaking into the President's office and hand-to-hand combat. The action is non-stop from the moment the resistance breaks into the defence bunker on Mars. 'I know that when we did take over the bunker I was basically playing Lyta as f**king terrified,' recalls actress Patricia Tallman. 'Because that's not her role at all. There they are, blowing people up and wrestling around and taking over the bunker and she's going "oh my God!"'

'I've got memories of putting on a Panka, gas mask, gloves, boots and a huge jumpsuit in the middle of March out in the valley, eighty-five degrees,' adds Franklin actor Richard Biggs. 'That was pretending that it was freezing outside, that I'm on Mars.'

Within this display of heroics there are several moments of reflection that make the conflict come alive for the characters. For Franklin, it is the ethical issue of using the telepaths as weapons in a war. The Shadows altered them and made them into weapons components, but inside they are still Human and to use them in this way almost makes Franklin and the others as bad as the Shadows. It is a difficult concept for the doctor to accept, even though he knows that these thirty telepaths have the potential to stop a firefight that could kill thirty thousand. He has reconciled himself to the fact, but still feels the need to justify it to one of the resistance fighters in the bunker. It is a theme that is repeated throughout the fourth season. G'Kar must scream for Cartagia to put himself in a position to save his people, Cartagia must be killed to free Centauri Prime and Sheridan must take up arms against his own government if Clark's massacres of civilians are to be stopped. 'There's no question that sometimes war does require of you actions that under other circumstances might be considered questionable,' says Joe Straczynski. 'That's one of the terrible things about war, it isn't a clean process. Too often war is dealt with in a jingoistic fashion and every so often you have to say "no it changes us and makes us do things that we don't necessarily want to do, that we have no choice but to do".'

The episode is peppered with visual references to different films which John Copeland used as an inspiration for the look of some scenes. Some of the classics are reflected in the scenes of telepaths waking up on the Earth destroyers and climbing out of their cryonic freezer units. 'That was the horror movie,' says John. 'We played with some Dutch angles and false perspectives as we dollied and moved and made one of the cryonic tubes come at us like Dracula's coffin when the lid cracks. It was just like a Hammer film at that moment. Playing with lurching shadows across the wall is like *Frankenstein*, stalking through the streets of the village on the way to grab the bride. It was really fun to do those kinds of things and it all came together into marvellously creepy sections.'

It is Lyta who wakes the telepaths, standing on the Martian surface looking towards the fleet of Earth destroyers, helping to disable them all one by one. 'She's again all alone,' laments Patricia. 'This is the last you see of her in the fourth season, all alone. Her eyes go black because she is communicating and controlling thirty telepaths in space, she has to control them, she doesn't want to let them go, she doesn't want to kill anybody. So once again she's saving everybody's butt – and they leave her there!'

The action increases with the battle over Mars and then the fight for Earth. President Clark, seeing that he is beaten, turns the defence platforms towards the planet in a final act to punish those who conspired against him. Sheridan's forces are in the right place at the right time to prevent the Earth being destroyed and, as the last platform turns towards North America, Sheridan's ship is the only one close enough to take action. It is severely damaged, its weapons systems do not work and so the only solution is to ram straight into it. Once again, Sheridan is prepared to die for what he believes in. 'That's the ultimate sacrificial hero,' says actor Bruce Boxleitner. 'That's Captain Ahab ready to climb on top of the whale himself and willing to die along with it. It's crazy, suicidal. He wants to go out in a big way. He has this thing for pyrotechnics, he's slightly the mad bomber, he really is. When in doubt, blow it up!'

The battle sequences themselves were a challenge for Captain Action. The fight is between two fleets of identical ships and that meant intercutting between two different bridge crews who had to be filmed on the same set. 'There was a challenge there to make them feel like two different kind of places,' says John Copeland. 'Two different places mentally for the people who were there, from the Clark EarthGov ideology and from the guys coming home to free Earth. [The director of photography] John Flinn and I talked about that quite a bit, both tonally in the lighting and in the way we moved the camera around. We showed different things on the *Apollo* than we showed on the *Aggy*, and we actually got quite daring on some of the things. I loved some of the photography that we did on the bridge of the *Aggy*, you really feel like it's *The Hunt for Red October* with Bruce, and moving through layers of screens with things going on. Of course, when the *Aggy* gets hammered to pieces in the fight for the platforms on Earth, we just blow the shit out of it. That was very cool because I got to blow up a lot of fun stuff and send guys flying through partitions and have ceilings collapse on people and send a girder up through the floor. What I wanted to do was try to show a different kind of damage to what we usually do to the sets, so it felt like the ship was getting massively crunched from all sides. You can do that in any kind of a ship that's got decks and levels to it, but we'd never gone to that extent before.'

It was clearly a rewarding experience to be let loose on such an action-packed episode. John went from the producer often seen on set looking at the time ticking away on his pocket watch, to being right in the middle of it. And, just like with Stephen Furst's directorial début, it was a chance for cast and crew to have some fun at his expense. 'Everyone was doing their bit with their watch,' says John. 'I had that done to me innumerable times, including by Joe. It was a wonderfully fun experience. People would come out to tease me and they would say "why are you smiling so much? You're having too good a time!"'

The episode is very much about the battle for Earth, but after such an adrenaline-rush, it ends with a very tender moment with Marcus finally confessing to Ivanova that he loves her. 'It was very tough, that "I love you",' says actor Jason Carter, 'because contained in that "I love you" is a commitment to everything, your entire life is in those words, so there is a tremendous responsibility.'

It was not made easier for him by Claudia Christian's less-than-sorrowful mood on the day. '[It was] "lie down, Claudia, please, you're supposed to be almost dead!"' Jason recalls with a smile. '"Please Claudia, please lie down, I've got to get into this kind of thing". It was hard, but the audience will know whether I got there. It's not a casual "I love you" when you're giving her your entire life. Powerful stuff.'

21:
'Rising Star'

The newscaster looks up nervously. 'Hello,' she says, almost surprised that she is back on ISN after so long under Clark's control. In a faltering voice that steadily gets stronger, she tells of the battle for Earth, Clark's suicide and Sheridan's surrender. 'Despite Sheridan's current high standing in public opinion polls, his decision to act against his fellow officers must be explained and justified.'

Franklin rushes back to Babylon 5 where he finds Ivanova sitting on the floor of Medlab, crying. Marcus made the ultimate sacrifice for her; he gave away the last of his life energy, ensuring he would die instead of her. 'Why did he have to do it?' she asks. 'I never would've asked him to...'

Sheridan stands to attention as the new President of Earth enters. She tells him he has no choice but to resign from EarthForce. 'The bitch of it is, you probably did the right thing,' says President Luchenko. 'But you did it the wrong way... and you have to pay the penalty for that.'

A group of men in a warehouse on Mars gather around to see the small plastic box that has been delivered to the door. One of them opens it, it starts smoking and he instinctively drops it on the floor. The box explodes and the room is filled with smoke. Garibaldi and a group of Rangers break down the door and dispatch the men with a flurry of fighting pikes, fists and PPGs. Garibaldi runs off down the hallway calling out for Lise. He hears her on the inside of one of the doors and fires at the lock, kicks the door down and leads her to safety.

Sheridan makes his resignation speech in front of news cameras that are relaying it live around the world. Delenn then takes the stand and puts forward her vision for a new interstellar alliance of races. There is a gigantic boom outside and the White Star fleet flies in, casting shadows over the listening dignitaries. 'Their goal is to create the peace,' Delenn tells them. 'This is an economic and political alliance, not one based on military strength. The gains you will achieve by working peacefully with other races far outweigh anything you might achieve by force.' President Luchenko is uncertain about the benefits and neutrality of the Alliance, but Londo and G'Kar persuade her otherwise, especially as they plan to appoint a Human as the Alliance President – former captain, John Sheridan.

Sheridan enters the hallway outside his debriefing room on Earth and sees Delenn. She holds out her hand and from round the corner steps Sheridan's father. He stops for a moment, he can hardly believe it, then he steps forward and embraces his dad with relief.

Garibaldi sits up in bed watching ISN. 'He freed Mars. Can you believe it? He really did it,' he says to Lise who is lying beside him. She pulls him back under the covers and the news continues talking to itself in the background.

G'Kar sits with Londo in the White Star conference room, picking the rice and confetti from Sheridan and Delenn's wedding off his breast plate. 'They're quite a couple, aren't they?' Londo remarks. 'Almost makes you wish you could peek in at them, see how it's going, doesn't it?' G'Kar just smiles at Londo who notices his prosthetic eye is missing. It lies instead on top of the dresser in Sheridan and Delenn's room, quietly watching them sleeping peacefully in each other's arms.

Episode titles have charted *Babylon 5*'s descent into darkness from Season Two, with 'A Race Through Dark Places' through to 'The Long Twilight Struggle' and 'The Fall of Night'. Season Four begins by getting darker still with 'The Hour of the Wolf' and 'The Long Night' then emerging into dawn with 'Between the Darkness and the Light' and eventually into the first rays of sunlight with 'Rising Star'. A sense of hope extends over the whole episode with the gathering together of all races to form an alliance for peace.

But the great victory is not without cost and within this spirit of hope lies a sense of grief over Marcus's death. It creates a deep mental scar for Ivanova who has to live with the fact that she only survived because he sacrificed himself for her. It is something she expresses to Franklin in a simple, but moving scene. 'It was great, I wish I'd had more scenes like that,' says actress Claudia Christian. 'That was very tragic. The enormous amount of guilt, the guilt was overwhelming, and that's why I said I didn't want him to do it. I think it was just horrifying for somebody to give up his life for her, and then more horrifying to think of how she treated him.'

However, Marcus's death was not entirely certain, even during the filming of this episode. Two versions were actually filmed, the first where he dies and the second where he is put into cryonic suspension on the point of death in the hope that he might be revived in the future. 'I wasn't sure myself what I wanted to do in that case,' admits writer Joe Straczynski. 'I just didn't want to kill off the character, I was very fond of Marcus and I was giving myself room to cut in either direction. My final decision came from the fact that, look, Ivanova's put herself on the line at one point and was ready to die and if I do a second cheat – or what appears to be a cheat – by pulling Marcus out of the fire at the last moment, does that undermine and diminish what he just did? And finally, in great distress about the whole thing, I realized that no, I have to do this right.'

Much of this episode is wrapping up the loose ends in preparation for what many people thought would be the end of the series, while still leaving the door open in case a Fifth Season was forthcoming. 'Rising Star' sees the greater issues of the future of Earth and the alliance resolved, and at the same time brings more personal matters to a satisfactory close.

For Garibaldi, that means rescuing Lise. 'There's a good outtake on that one,' says actor Jerry Doyle. 'They had all these cells built with these solid doors with all these big steel locks on them. I had to come down the hall and start kicking doors open. In rehearsal they had just tacked them on the back with maybe a single screw and I said "it's just not good". So they ended up with a couple of the special effects guys behind the door and that was supposed to be the resistance. As they felt the kick, they would back off and the door would open and show she's not in there. John Flinn just got me up to speed before I came round the corner, "remember where you were, remember where you were", and I go "right, right, right". I came round the corner, I kicked this door and the special effects guy goes flying off the set, the door coming off the hinges and I go "where's the next one?" So now I'm in a full frenzy, trying to find her and I go to kick this one door and I'm kicking and kicking – what had happened was the real steel lock had engaged, so I'm trying to kick down the entire set! I'm kicking and I'm kicking and now I'm throwing my shoulder into it, and the crew's just watching me and I'm screaming her name. Finally I see the door pop open towards me and I go "Lise?" I just pulled open the door opposite to the way I was trying to kick it in!'

Once Lise is rescued, now that her husband is dead, it leaves room for Garibaldi to be with her at last, and they discuss marriage during an intimate bed scene. 'They had it set up very nice with the candles and real dim lights,' Jerry remembers. 'She came out and we were basically both naked to get onto the set. It's a little weird walking around with seventy-five people watching, but John Flinn runs a very good set – the director too – and he said "OK, they're coming on set" and everybody just bailed, gave us a chance to get under the covers, get comfortable, and then they came back in. We have such a wonderful crew that it's an honour to work with them and for them. I love going to work, especially when you get to lie in bed for a couple of hours with a great-looking girl and you get paid for it. I'll do that anytime.'

For G'Kar and Londo, there is a sense of reconciliation as they sit down together and reflect upon the marriage of Sheridan and Delenn. 'G'Kar still has some issues to work out and Londo does too, but they are certainly at a resting point with each other,' says Londo actor Peter Jurasik. 'We also had a ball doing it. People who have seen Andreas live [on stage] know that he's a total nut. While he has Peter Brook and classic theatre on his resumé, he should really be a low-class vaudeville comedian. A circus performer is somewhere in his blood and he really made the scene a lot of fun for me to do.'

'I think a lot of the walls that had separated them had come tumbling down,' adds Andreas Katsulas, who plays G'Kar. 'But I suspect that G'Kar will always be a little cautious. He will go as far as he thinks it's possible to go. When you see how far we've come, how many episodes it took us, how many years it has taken to get the two of them just to that point where they're sitting there at the table and enjoying something together – boy, that's development.'

The marriage of Sheridan and Delenn is not played out in a scene of its own, instead the sense of love and commitment between them is expressed in a short bedroom scene. 'Wedding bliss!' says Bruce Boxleitner.

And it would be a fairytale ending if it weren't for G'Kar's prosthetic eye. Cinderella never had the wicked witch spying on her honeymoon with Prince Charming. 'I liked that. Joe can be a naughty boy,' says actress Mira Furlan. 'Joe didn't allow that scene to stand on its own. He included this evil and cynical commentary, this side story with G'Kar and Londo. That's good because with this romantic aspect, there's always the danger of being too melodramatic and too sweet. In this way, yes they are finally together lying in this bed, they love each other, they have conquered this evil in the universe, but there is this nasty little element, this cynical little joke with G'Kar which kind of puts it on Human ground.'

Delenn's marriage to Sheridan takes her one more step away from Lennier who has long held a secret love for her. There is a reminder of this in a small, but poignant moment in which Delenn denies that all love is unrequited. For Lennier, of course, that is precisely what it is and will always be. 'That was a powerful little scene and I thought that was quite possibly the last scene I'd ever shoot as Lennier,' says Bill Mumy. 'I was very moved by that scene, for more than one reason. The underlying stuff with Lennier, I don't think he wants to say to Delenn "I wish you wouldn't be with Sheridan, I wish you would be with me", I don't think he's happy, but he's accepted it and he wants what's best for her and he knows where her heart is. But nonetheless it is a hard cross to bear, to look at somebody who doesn't quite understand the fact that they are your world. So there was just the natural thought of Lennier in playing that scene, but there was also the thought from me, well the cameras are rolling and this may be the last ever time I speak for this character. It was a very emotional moment. I think I might have even have cried a little bit.'

22:
'The Deconstruction of Falling Stars'

*Confetti showers down on Sheridan and Delenn as
they walk onto Babylon 5 for the first time since
their wedding. Londo looks unhappily at the
celebrations which, on his world, would be for a
funeral. 'This is a very bad sign for the future,' he
says.*

*One hundred years later and historians are
analysing President Sheridan's actions. They believe
many of the stories surrounding Sheridan and
Delenn are pure myth. They say he had a 'good PR
machine' that covered up mistakes such as that
which precipitated the telepath war. But their
discussion is interrupted by Delenn, now one
hundred and forty years old. They look on in awe at
the old woman, her face now haggard and wrinkled.
'He was a good man,' she says slowly, but
deliberately. 'A kind man who cared about the
world even when the world cared nothing for him.'*

*It's five hundred years since Sheridan set up the
Alliance, and Earth is at war with itself. One half
wants to break away from the Alliance and has
constructed a holographic representation of Babylon
5 which it plans to broadcast to the whole of
Humanity. Accurate holographic copies of Sheridan,
Delenn, Franklin and Garibaldi – complete with
their memories and thought patterns – shimmer into
existence. They are made to play out fictional
scenarios which discredit the foundations on which
the Alliance was based, but Garibaldi's hologram*

suggests to the programmer that he can offer something better. He was Sheridan's strategic planner during the war and could offer that same service in their conflict too. The programmer says their plan is to make the first strike against the enemy, targeting civilian populations to force a surrender. Garibaldi smiles and reveals their whole conversation has been broadcast to the enemy. A warning siren wails as missiles head their way and the programmer runs out in terror. The missiles hit, obliterating his holographic creation in a blast of energy.

One thousand years on and tales of Sheridan and the Alliance are but legends. Earth has been decimated by war and its technology destroyed in the Great Burn of five centuries ago. One young monk has dedicated his life to rediscovering Humanity's lost knowledge, but is having a crisis of faith. Earth's only hope lies in the prophecy of Delenn III who said Rangers would come from the heavens in their hour of need, but it has been so long and they have not come. Brother Alwyn suggests the Rangers might already be here, working secretly where those who fear their scientific knowledge will not notice them. The young monk, somewhat reassured, leaves and Brother Alwyn takes his Ranger costume from the wardrobe. 'We will rebuild the Earth,' he says to himself, 'but this time we will build it better.'

One million years later and the Earth's sun is on the brink of death. One man who has elected to stay behind sends all the records of Human history to New Earth by tachyon relay with the words: 'You will live on, the voices of our ancestors... We created the world we think you would have wished for us. Now we leave the cradle for the last time.'

His Human form turns into energy and enters a suit that resembles one the Vorlons once used. Out in space, the sun explodes in a ball of fire.

In 2262 Sheridan lies in bed with Delenn wondering if what they did will be remembered in a thousand years' time. She tells him they did what they did because it was right, not to be remembered. 'History,' she says, 'will tend to itself.'

'The Deconstruction of Falling Stars' was a last-minute addition to Season Four. The original twenty-second episode filmed for the fourth season was 'Sleeping in Light', an episode set twenty years into the future designed to be the final ever episode of *Babylon 5*. It was written and filmed after US cable channel TNT eventually saved the day by stepping in at the eleventh hour to order a fifth season from Warner Bros. J. Michael Straczynski therefore got the fifth season for the show that he had always planned to last five years. 'Sleeping in Light' was pulled from the fourth season and saved for the end of the fifth to provide a proper end for the series, as was originally envisaged. In its place came 'The Deconstruction of Falling Stars' which was the first episode filmed in Season Five. It explains the final on-screen message: 'Dedicated to all the people who predicted that the Babylon project would fail in its mission. Faith manages.'

All this happened after the interviews for this book had taken place and after most of it had been written. It is, therefore, not possible to include a full discussion of 'The Deconstruction of Falling Stars' in this volume. It will appear, instead, as a bonus chapter in the forthcoming *Babylon 5: Season by Season* guide #5.